AIR FORCE FELLOWS

COLLEGE OF AEROSPACE DOCTRINE, RESEARCH AND EDUCATION

AIR UNIVERSITY

Transnational Crime and the Criminal-Terrorist Nexus
Synergies and Corporate Trends

JENNIFER L. HESTERMAN
Colonel, USAF

Walker Paper No. 1

Air University Press
Maxwell Air Force Base, Alabama 36112-6615

May 2005

Air University Library Cataloging Data

Hesterman, Jennifer L.
    Transnational crime and the criminal-terrorist nexus : synergies and corporate trends / Jennifer L. Hesterman.
        p. ; cm. – (Walker paper, 1555-7871 ; no. 1)
    Includes bibliographical references.

        1. Transnational crime. 2. Terrorism—Finance. 3. Terrorists—Social networks. 4. Organized crime. I. Title. II. Series.

    364.135—dc22

Disclaimer

This Walker Paper and others in the series are available electronically at the Air University Research Web site http://research.maxwell.af.mil and the AU Press Web site http://aupress.maxwell.af.mil.

Since 1958 the Air Force has assigned a small number of carefully chosen, experienced officers to serve one-year tours at distinguished civilian institutions studying national security policy and strategy. Beginning with the 1994 academic year, these programs were accorded senior service school professional military education in-residence credit. In 2003 these fellowships assumed senior developmental education (SDE), force development credit for eligible officers.

The SDE-level Air Force Fellows serve as visiting military ambassadors to their centers, devoting effort to expanding their colleagues' understanding of defense matters. As such, candidates for SDE-level fellowships have a broad knowledge of key DOD and Air Force issues. SDE-level fellows perform outreach by their presence and voice in sponsoring institutions. SDE-level fellows are expected to provide advice, promote, and explain Air Force and DOD policies, programs, and military doctrine strategy to nationally recognized scholars, foreign dignitaries, and leading policy analysts. The AF Fellows also gain valuable perspectives from the exchange of ideas with these civilian leaders. SDE-level fellows are expected to apprise appropriate Air Force agencies of significant developments and emerging views on defense and economic and foreign policy issues within their centers. Each fellow is expected to use the unique access she or he has as grounds for research and writing on important national security issues. The SDE AF Fellows include the National Defense Fellows, the RAND Fellows, the National Security Fellows, and the Secretary of Defense Corporate Fellows. In addition, the Air Force Fellows supports a post-SDE military fellow at the Council on Foreign Relations.

On the intermediate developmental education level, the chief of staff approved several AF Fellowships focused on career broadening for Air Force majors. The Air Force Legislative

Fellows was established in April 1995 with the Foreign Policy Fellowship and Defense Advanced Research Projects Agency Fellowship coming under the AF Fellows program in 2003. In 2004, the AF Fellows also assumed responsibility of the National Laboratories Technologies Fellows.

Contents

Table

Foreword

As we address security challenges at home and abroad, America faces several threats to its security that alone are concerning; taken together, they demand our immediate action. The once-clear lines between the international drug trade, terrorism, and organized crime are now blurring, crossing, and mutating as never before.

The US government has made great strides in the post-9/11 era and is quickly coming to grips with this modern phenomenon. Our nation's leaders now better understand its roots and have taken significant actions to address the multitude of threats we face today. For example, US efforts to secure our borders from terrorists have yielded not only counterterrorism but also counternarcotic successes, as drug seizures have increased dramatically since 9/11. But this is not a war that can be won overnight; it will require continued vigilance and innovative tactics to counter a threat that adapts its actions based on our successes. We cannot afford to march into the future backwards.

Addressing the convergence of organized crime, drug trafficking, and terrorism requires the new paradigm of strategic thinking that the war on terrorism has ushered in. As we now understand such an effort cannot be seen through a diplomatic, military, law enforcement, financial, or intelligence lens alone. Rather, it demands a prism of all of these to offer a comprehensive and coordinated approach.

Colonel Hesterman's analysis of this subject is accurate and timely. She provides a fresh look at the criminal/terrorist nexus and by examining corporate trends, provides unique insights into funding aspects of both activities. This important subject matter is ripe for further policy and substantive analytical focus. Analysts and policy makers alike can certainly use her study's conclusions and recommendations in their efforts to protect our nation against this vexing threat.

FRANK J. CILLUFFO
Director
Homeland Security Policy Institute
The George Washington University

About the Author

Col Jennifer L. Hesterman

Col Jennifer L. Hesterman was born in Latrobe, Pennsylvania, and was commissioned in 1986 as a graduate of Air Force ROTC at Pennsylvania State University. Her initial assignment was to Moody AFB, Georgia, where she spent three years serving in a variety of positions and was named Tactical Air Command Administration Officer of the Year in 1988. In 1989 she was selected for special duty with the F-117A Stealth Fighter program at Tonopah Test Range, Nevada, and served as assistant chief, Combat Plans; flight chief, Logistics Plans; and commander, 37th Logistics Support Squadron. In 1992 she was reassigned to the Air Force District of Washington, first to the Military Personnel Flight, then, in 1993, to the Office of the Secretary of the Air Force, Legislative Liaison, where she worked and traveled with members of Congress and their staff. In 1996 she assumed command of the 48th Mission Support Squadron, Royal Air Force Lakenheath, United Kingdom, and was named USAFE Senior Personnel Manager of the Year in 1997. After completing Air Command and Staff College at Maxwell AFB, Alabama, she transitioned back to the Pentagon in 1999 and served as chief, Air Force Retirement and Separation Policy. In 2001 she assumed the role of deputy commander, 4th Support Group, Seymour Johnson AFB, North Carolina, and ultimately commanded the group for six months. In 2002 Colonel Hesterman was reassigned to the Pentagon as executive officer to the Air Force deputy chief of staff, Personnel. Following her selection as a National Defense

Fellow in 2003, she undertook a year of study at the Center for Strategic and International Studies, International Security Program, in Washington DC. Colonel Hesterman assumed her current position as chief, Assignment Policy and Procedures Division, Air Force Personnel Center, Randolph Air Force Base, Texas, in June 2004. She holds Master of Science degrees in applied behavioral science (emphasis in organizational development) from the Johns Hopkins University and military operational art from Air University. She is married to Col John Hesterman, and they have a daughter, Sarah.

Preface

Like all Americans, the 9/11 terrorist attacks were a crystallizing event in my life. I found myself in the unexpected position of trying to secure a major military installation and its panicked residents from an unknown enemy with unknown intentions and unknown capability. Along with my stunned colleagues, I watched the defense readiness condition (DEF-CON) change, indicating that our country was under attack. Information from the staff came at a blinding pace: unknown persons on the base perimeter, an unidentifiable inbound helicopter, suspicious packages, and a man of Middle Eastern appearance at the gate without identification. In the midst of the confusion, we received word that the president was airborne—our base in North Carolina was his second landing choice. Were we ready?

The following day, federal law-enforcement officials informed us they had infiltrated a local cell of Hezbollah sympathizers who were smuggling cigarettes and, for unknown reasons, had purchased night vision goggles and stun guns. The proximity of the terrorist threat to my base and its populace was chilling. As the case unfolded, I learned firsthand of the emerging, deadly connections between organized crime and terrorism. This body of research for the Institute for National Security Studies was a continuation of my interest and self-study of this subject. To add a "voice" to my research, I spoke off-the-record with many law-enforcement agents involved in the unglamorous work of chasing the terrorist money trail. Underresourced and overtasked, they work with unbelievable dedication, hoping to prevent further attacks. This study is dedicated to them, the unsung heroes of the war on terror.

JENNIFER L. HESTERMAN
Colonel, USAF

Abstract

Modernized transnational crime is on the rise and threatens our national security like never before. Globalization, technological advances, and anarchy resulting from the end of the Cold War has made transnational crime much easier to perpetrate and has given criminals flexibility to change tactics to evade law enforcement continually. Exacerbating the growing problem is the fact that the groups involved in transnational crime operate with a level of sophistication previously only found in multinational corporations. Eurasian transnational crime is considered by government agencies as the most worrisome and largest threat to the United States because of its size, wealth, and global reach. The problem of human trafficking is expanding throughout Eurasia and the Baltic nations and has now reached our shores. An emerging area of concern is the region surrounding a corrupt North Korea, as it expands its influence beyond its borders.

Many agencies are involved in the fight against transnational crime and cite progress in capacity-building efforts with other nations to establish and enforce the rule of law. These engagement activities will also help stem corruption, which aggravates transnational crime.

Factoring terrorist groups into the mix complicates the problem. The prospects of the potential synergy and mere seductive nature of this liaison are frightening and have dire implications. The criminal-terrorist nexus exists in many ways, whether through direct liaison or in copying "business" operations and tactics. Terrorists' fund-raising methods can be as sophisticated as those found in multinational corporations, as they seek to earn, move, and store their assets. Narco-terrorism is a good example of the partnering of organized crime with terrorists, and Afghanistan and Colombia corner the global market on drugs (and terror). Criminals and terrorists both engage in money-laundering activities, although the tactics and goals vary. An emerging area of concern is intellectual property crime, or the counterfeiting and pirating of goods that are then manufactured and sold for profit without the consent of the patent or trademark holder. This activity is more lucrative than drug trafficking, is less pursued by law-enforcement agencies, and the penalties if caught and prosecuted are far less severe than those for other criminal activities.

The US State Department has issued four trends in international terrorist groups: decline in state-sponsored terror, move to loosely affiliated groups, a shift in tactics, and alliance with transnational crime. These trends can be studied through the lens of terror financing to predict future business activities and the "corporate trend" in terrorism.

Much research has been done on transnational crime and terrorist financing; however, the intersection of the two requires more study, as this "battle at the crossroads" requires new approaches. Asymmetric engagement and use of "soft" instruments of power are essential. The use of containment and deterrence, strategies that policy makers typically do not find appealing, are necessary in this new realm as we try to marginalize the threat and decrease the playing field. Scholarly study regarding the life cycle of modern terrorist groups may yield clues as to when and why, despite their religious ideology, they partner with organized crime.

More expertise in the field of financial forensics is crucial, with practitioners educated on both organized crime and terrorist-funding tactics. Powers bestowed on federal law-enforcement agencies through the Patriot Act must be upheld to help fight modern organized crime and terrorism in the global environment, and agents require expanded training on proactive, investigative approaches to stop crime and terrorist acts before they happen, not merely to analyze the outcome, as is the traditional procedure. Government agencies are effectively sharing information at the tactical level. Strategic-level interaction is weak and requires attention. With greater education and training on these issues, the US military could be a powerful force multiplier. This study academically frames the issue, providing policy makers a fresh perspective on existing and emerging threats to use in their future planning and modeling efforts.

Chapter 1

"A Poisonous Brew"

While organized crime is not a new phenomenon today, some governments find their authority besieged at home and their foreign policy interests imperiled abroad. Drug trafficking, links between drug traffickers and terrorists, smuggling of illegal aliens, massive financial and bank fraud, arms smuggling, potential involvement in the theft and sale of nuclear material, political intimidation, and corruption all constitute a poisonous brew—a mixture potentially as deadly as what we faced during the Cold War.

—R. James Woolsey
Former Director, CIA

R. James Woolsey's quote should serve as a wake-up call not only to the United States but also to countries around the world. Transnational organized crime is escalating, and the synergistic potential of the alliance between organized crime and terrorists is alarming. The twenty-first century is five years old, and already the world has experienced extreme acts of terror resulting in death and destruction exceeding those witnessed in the previous 20 years. Besides fanatical ideology, what is fueling these terrorist groups? And how can they continue to operate with such abandon despite an all-out effort to fight the global war on terror? One answer may be the corresponding rise in transnational crime. Globally, drug-trafficking routes are robust and plenty; the ghastly business of human trafficking is flourishing; and money is laundered in amounts and ways never before imagined. Many resource-constrained countries struggle to deal with their role in this epidemic and are attempting to contain it. Others are corrupt and choose to look the other way, or worse, benefit from illicit activity. Our government continues to spend a staggering $1 billion annually to help other countries identify and battle their transnational crimes issues. Why?

Transnational crime is an emerging and growing US national security threat, and it threatens us in new, provoking ways. For example, Americans formerly viewed drug use as a law-enforcement or health issue. Only recently has drug trafficking been established as a global crime with a corresponding national security threat. A lesser-known and understood example of a growing transnational threat reaching our borders is human trafficking. Unbeknownst to many, our national security strategy contains a goal labeled "Champion Aspirations for Human Dignity."[1] When a boat filled with women and children leaves the shores of a distant country delivering them to a life of enslavement and unimaginable abuse, we obviously feel compelled to engage out of moral obligation and belief that human dignity must be upheld and supported. If 18,000–20,000 of those human beings are delivered annually by criminals to the United States and forced into prostitution, pornography, and sweatshop labor, it becomes an obvious and direct threat to the fabric of our society.[2] Add terrorists to the equation—using established and often unchallenged trafficking routes as a logistics trail—and the issue takes on new significance.

Transnational crime also threatens allies we have vowed to assist and protect; a challenge to their security and strength directly impacts the United States. Many nation-states are on the brink of thriving or failing, and their fate depends either on us or on the help of organized crime and terrorists. History reveals that failing countries are like dominoes: they lead to failing regions, an even greater threat to our national security.

To fully grasp this complex issue, it is first necessary to understand the multinational-corporate sophistication of the criminal groups involved in transnational crime. This study reviews regions by scope in addition to a variety of criminal activity. Adding further context is an overview of US agencies involved, methods used, and lessons learned in the fight against transnational crime—all of which could be applied to the global war on terror. Factoring the terrorist element into the issue and explaining the resulting nexus clarifies the urgency of this threat. This discussion addresses known and emerging methods of financing terror that have equivalent transnational and corporate aspects to organized transnational crime, which allows visibility into ongoing or potential alliances. The study culminates by addressing trends in international terrorist groups that affect their corporateness as they evolve and change in light of the global war on terror.

Notes

Most of the notes for this chapter and the following chapters appear in shortened form. For full details, see the appropriate entries in the bibliography.

1. National Security Council, "Champion Aspirations for Human Dignity."
2. Department of State, "Trafficking in Persons Report."

Chapter 2

Transnational Crime

Transnational organized crime has been likened to a cancer, spreading across the world. It can undermine democracy, disrupt free markets, drain national assets, and inhibit the development of stable societies. In doing so, national and international criminal groups threaten the security of all nations.

—Department of State

The concept of transnational crime is not new. Money, drugs, and commodities have always been smuggled across borders and oceans as criminals circumvented laws to enhance their illicit activity. However, modern transnational crime is a recent phenomenon and is far deadlier, more expansive, and extremely difficult to infiltrate. According to the United Nations (UN), the threat posed by transnational organized crime to the political, economic, and social fabric of societies appeared in the mid-1990s. Aggravating factors include globalization of business networks, lowered trade barriers, technological advances, and anarchy caused by the end of the Cold War. These dynamics have also contributed to the rise of a new class of actors who operate outside the traditional nation-state system, which makes detection, intervention, and prevention very challenging.

Transnational crime is penetrating our society in new and dangerous ways. Grant D. Ashley, assistant director of the Criminal Investigative Division at the Federal Bureau of Investigation (FBI), testified, "It is our belief that the international growth of these very dangerous, criminally diverse and organized groups and their emergence in the United States has caused a significant expansion of our crime problem."[1] This expansion could obviously be used as a vehicle by terrorists to move resources, recruit, or simply spread their sphere of influence. To successfully engage this enemy abroad and at home and to effectively dismantle their operations, agencies must understand how, where, and why these criminals operate.

5

Multinational Corporate Sophistication

Although routinely underestimated in relation to sophistication, transnational criminal organizations act as networks and pursue the same types of joint ventures and strategic alliances as legitimate multinational corporations. A multinational corporation is often defined as one that operates on a worldwide scale and without ties to any specific nation or region. The global business environment is unique and multifaceted, which requires extra considerations. Because of the complexity of international operations, the right people (e.g., lawyers, accountants, and subject-area experts) must be on the payroll. Analysis of the international customer base, product demand, and proper positioning of the product is necessary to maximize profit. The company must assess the cost of doing business and streamline staff and operational activities, thus cutting costs as much as possible. Any business must have good supply-chain management, from procurement to storage to product delivery. This process requires extra planning and sophistication when applied to a global market. Understanding international commerce laws and issues related to the operation of offshore businesses is a necessity. Cultural knowledge of the countries involved in the transactions is necessary, including languages, currencies, and business practices; the corporate strategy must be in sync with these cultural nuances. All savvy business ventures are low risk or high return, and most are able to extract profits throughout the process. A good international business is able to leverage rapidly changing communication and transportation technology to stay viable.[2]

The above could have easily been a description of the Cali Cartel drug syndicate at its peak in the late 1980s. Successful international criminal enterprises follow the same business plan and often work in parallel with unsuspecting legitimate corporations by using their business practices as a model. They have the right people on the payroll who know how to maximize profits and who can shift strategies as technology evolves or when detected by law enforcement. They are well resourced. Many organizations own and operate a variety of aircraft and boats, with skilled operators at the helm. Sophisticated satellite phones and use of Global Positioning System equipment keep the criminals on the run and investigators in the dark. Unfortunately for governments battling this issue, not only are transnational criminal networks harder to detect and infiltrate than ever before; despite their best efforts, business is booming.

Transnational Organized Crime on the Rise

There are several categories of crime and criminals. The FBI defines organized crime as "a continuing criminal conspiracy having a firm organizational structure, a conspiracy fed by fear and corruption."[3] Although organized crime is typically associated with the mafia or drug trafficking, it extends to any continuing criminal enterprise such as money laundering or white-collar crime. Reactive crimes are violent or nonviolent crimes perpetrated by an individual or a small group, such as burglaries, Internet crime, and hate crimes. There are also crimes of opportunity, such as pickpocketing or a lone carjacking, in which the criminal targets the easiest mark or acts because of the target's carelessness. Although any of the above methods could generate resources, transnational criminal and global terrorist organizations are more likely to affiliate with the continuing criminal enterprise. Therefore, the focus in this study is on organized crime.

Several factors contribute to the existence and proliferation of transnational organized crime originating, traversing, or being committed in a country. One major consideration is available resources, whether a shared ideology, a desperate populace, a weak economy, or geographical or geological features. Border security and strength of the rule of law are critical and will either repel or attract transnational criminal activity. A weak government invites penetration by organized crime, and the resulting corruption further delegitimizes the country's government. Terrorists are also thriving in several regions, which exacerbates existing crime problems.

The extent and global impact of transnational crime emerged in 2003 when State Department and FBI officials were called to testify to Congress regarding its increase. This study uses their testimony, along with that of other experts, to explore the hotbeds of existing and emerging transnational crime.

Eurasian Transnational Crime Most Worrisome

According to the FBI, Eurasian organized crime poses some of the greatest threats because of its size, wealth, and global reach. Eurasian organized crime is associated with Russia, Eastern and Central European countries, and the independent states formed after the fall of the Soviet Union. Although a victory for democracy, the demise of communism and the resulting leadership void caused great economic and social chaos that allowed for the rise of many organized crime groups. Civil wars are still unresolved, and corruption is widespread.

According to a 2003 General Accounting Office report that studied interagency programs that fight transnational crime, the US government is concerned about the unique blend of circumstances in Eurasia. Terrorism, international organized crime, trafficking in persons and drugs, ethnic separatism, religious extremism, and corruption are present and thriving.[4]

Corruption of government officials in Eurasian countries is a main concern and contributes to the proliferation of transnational crime in this region. In testimony to the US Senate in 2003, Steven Pifer, deputy assistant secretary of state in the Bureau of European and Eurasian Affairs at the State Department, expertly described how a vacuum in institutions leads to corruption.

> The process of privatization of vast state resources often took place in the absence of any effective legal or regulatory structure, and many valuable state assets were privatized in "insider transactions." As a result, property rights were unclear, and disputes over property rights often could not be resolved in courts of law. Insiders and organized crime took advantage of this situation to take control of major assets, often having to pay no more than a small fraction of their true value. Privatization took place roughly simultaneously with the development of small-scale private businesses.

> Again, because of the absence of an effective legal and regulatory system governing the activity of private enterprises, these businesses were ripe for extortion by street gangs. In order to protect themselves, small businesses often had to turn to other gangsters to provide a "krysha" (roof) of protection. Consequently, gangsters gained control of many small businesses and accumulated capital, which they frequently used to acquire larger businesses during the privatization process. They often then used these businesses to make more money and to acquire public status, which they then used to obtain political office.[5]

Unfortunately, this scenario is playing out in numerous countries around the world, and use of this historical example should be incorporated in post-conflict reconstruction and democratization planning. Rapidly establishing and enforcing the rule of law following governmental upheaval are essential to prevent a haven for criminals and terrorists.

In terms of individual countries, the organized crime problem in Russia is perhaps the most pressing. According to Steve Schrage, deputy assistant secretary for International Narcotics and Law Enforcement Affairs (INL) at the State Department, the Russian interior ministry estimated that more than one-half of the Russian economy, including significant portions of its vast energy and metallurgical sectors, is controlled by organized crime. In a country where by some accounts more than half the population earns less than $70 a month, he stated that this year alone, criminal groups in Russia have used Russian banks to illegally transfer $9 billion out of the country. The FBI believes that the wide range of criminal activity engaged in by Russian organized crime groups likely exceeds in scale and economic impact that of the Cali Cartel at the height of its power.[6]

According to the UN, all Eurasian countries are rife with human-trafficking violations. Human trafficking occurs when men, women, and children are procured, transported, and then enslaved. This form of slavery involves forced labor and sexual exploitation. Trafficking is aggravated by poverty and desire for a better life; lack of education as to the consequences by families and individuals; and disruption of societal values or, in other words, greed. Trafficking is a high-profit, low-risk industry. According to the State Department, many Eurasian countries are lagging in instituting and enforcing laws to punish perpetrators of trafficking.[7]

Another criminal activity prolific in the region includes significant money-laundering consortiums and schemes. The proximity of the golden crescent of Pakistan and Afghanistan puts Tajikistan, Uzbekistan, Kazakhstan, Turkmenistan, and Kyrgyzstan at the crossroads of the opiate trade to Europe and Russia, where narcotics consumption is increasing.[8]

9

Eurasian organized crime spread to the United States in the 1970s and 1980s with the arrival of more than 100,000 soviet émigrés. Mixed in with law-abiding people was a very small group of criminals that became the base of US domestic Eurasian organized crime. The dissolution of the Soviet Union in 1991 brought thousands more émigrés fleeing social strife and dismal economic conditions. This exodus added to the existing Eurasian criminal enterprise in the United States. According to the FBI, there are 245 ongoing cases dealing with Eurasian organized crime, with fraud constituting 60 percent of all cases. Other criminal activities attributed to Eurasian organized crime in the United States include transnational money laundering, extortion, drug trafficking, auto theft, white-slave-trafficking prostitution, hostage taking, extortion of immigrant celebrities and sports figures, transportation of stolen property for export, insurance (staged auto accidents) and medical fraud (false medical claims), counterfeiting, credit card forgery, and murder.[9] No crime is off limits to these groups, and the breadth and depth of their criminal activity is frustratingly astounding.

Italian Transnational Crime

Italian Organized Crime (IOC) groups are becoming transnational in nature. The best known of these groups is the Sicilian mafia, but other significant up-and-coming IOC groups include the Neapolitan camorra, the Calabrian 'ndrangheta, and the Puglian sacra corona unita. There is now open-source reporting regarding new connections between the US's domestic La Cosa Nostra (LCN) families and the Sicilian mafia, including international travel of members to meet. IOC factions continue to traffic drugs and launder money using the United States as a conduit. According to the INL, the Calabrian 'ndrangheta transitioned from kidnappings to drug trafficking and corruption of public officials to gain lucrative municipal contracts. The Neapolitan camorra is possibly expanding its criminal activity beyond its traditional extortion rackets to the business of smuggling counterfeit goods and nontaxed cigarettes. The camorra is attempting to interject into the legitimate economies of Eastern Europe, while the Puglian sacra corona unita is allegedly taking advantage of its geographic proximity to the Balkans to align itself with Balkan organized criminal groups engaged in arms and cigarette smuggling and trafficking in humans.[10] Therefore, once regionalized in scope, the IOCs are employing their unique form of criminal activity transnationally, and their expansion is cause for concern.

Baltic Transnational Crime

Balkan Organized Crime (BOC) describes activity emanating from Slovenia, Croatia, Serbia-Montenegro, Bosnia-Herzegovina, Albania, Kosovo, the former Yugoslav republic of Macedonia, and Greece. BOC is an emerging organized crime problem with significant transnational ramifications, and European nations now recognize that BOC is one of the greatest criminal threats they face. BOC controls upwards of 70 percent of the heroin market in some of the larger European nations; they are rapidly taking over human smuggling, prostitution, and car-theft rings.

According to the State Department, terrorists and Islamic extremist groups have already exploited inadequate border security and institutional weaknesses in the Balkans. Middle Eastern nongovernmental organizations identified as supporting terrorist activities are currently providing assistance to Islamic extremist groups in the region. Terrorists also exploit some European countries' liberal asylum laws, open land borders, and weaknesses in their investigative, prosecutorial, and procedural processes while using these countries as operational staging areas for international terrorist attacks.[11] Albania and Kosovo lie at the heart of the Balkan Route that links the golden crescent; this route is worth an estimated $400 billion a year and handles 80 percent of heroin destined for Europe.[12]

According to the INL, BOC groups, particularly those composed of ethnic Albanians, have expanded rapidly over the last decade throughout Europe and are gaining a foothold in the United States. Albanian organized crime groups in the United States have been involved in murders, bank and automated teller machine burglaries, passport and visa fraud, illegal gambling, weapons and narcotics trafficking, and extortion.[13] The FBI believes the Albanians have challenged the LCN for control of some traditional criminal activities in New York City. Albanian organized crime groups have also formed partnerships with certain mafia families to facilitate crimes and are known for acts of extreme violence.[14]

Asian Transnational Crime

In the early 1900s, signs of Asian criminal enterprises emerged in the United States with the onset of criminally influenced Chinese groups. These groups thrived in the United States, and new enterprises have developed with globalization, communications technology, and international travel. In the United States, Asian criminal enterprises have been identified in more than 50 metropolitan areas.

According to the FBI, traditional Asian criminal enterprises impacting the United States are groups organized by criminals predominantly from East and Southeast Asia, including members of Chinese, Korean, Japanese, Thai, Filipino, Cambodian, Laotian, and Vietnamese descent. However, other Asian criminal enterprises are now emerging as domestic and international threats, including groups from the South Pacific Island nations as well as organizations from Southwest Asia such as Pakistan, India, Afghanistan, Nepal, and Iran. These groups are described as very fluid and extremely mobile, easily adapting to changes and thus able to evade law enforcement. They have multilingual skills, can be highly sophisticated in their criminal operations, and are well financed. Some groups have commercialized their criminal activities into business firms of various sizes, from small family-run operations to large corporations.

The FBI also believes the criminal conduct engaged in by Asian criminal enterprises includes not only traditional racketeering activities normally associated with organized crime such as extortion, murder, kidnapping, illegal gambling, prostitution, and loan sharking but also international organized crime problems such as alien smuggling, heroin and methamphetamine drug trafficking, such financial frauds as illegal credit cards, theft of automobiles and computer chips, counterfeiting of computer and clothing products, and money laundering.[15]

Trends in Asian criminal enterprises include the cooperation of other criminal groups that cross ethnic and racial heritage lines. Maturing groups are now structuring their groups hierarchically to be more competitive, and the criminal activities they engage in are global in nature. More enterprises are engaging in white-collar crimes and are now commingling these illegal activities with legitimate business ventures.[16]

An emerging area of concern in the region is the Malaysian straits, an area of considerable established and uncontrolled organized crime. The Indonesian archipelago is a series of 17,000 islands—a vast amount of territory to govern, patrol, and enforce the rule of law. Human trafficking is rampant in Indonesia, largely because of the tens of millions of people mired in poverty, corrupt governments, and no related law enforcement. The region is subjected to sporadic violence created by a handful of separatists grouping with gangsters engaged in weapons smuggling, money laundering, and drug trafficking.

According to the State Department, these activities are also fueling international terrorist activity. Previously, most terrorist activity in East Asia was related to domestic political disputes, but now the area is home to several lethal international terrorist groups. Organizations with direct links to al-Qaeda were discovered in 2001 in Malaysia and Singapore, and their activities, movements, and connections now traverse the entire region. The al-Qaeda offshoot, Jemaah Islamiyah (JI) is responsible for many large bombings in the last few years, impacting the tourist market and affecting the region's economy. The Abu Sayyaf Group (ASG), an Islamic extremist organization in the Philippines, kidnapped two Americans and killed one of them in 2002. An ASG subsidiary, the Abu Haf al-Masri Brigades, emerged as a lethal new group, initiating hotel bombings in Malaysia and possibly executing the train bombings in Madrid. The United States remains concerned about Islamic extremists operating in and around western China who have received training, equipment, and inspiration from al-Qaeda, the Taliban, and others in Afghanistan.[17]

It appears that multinational terrorist organizations and networks are thriving in the Malaysian straits region and operate unchallenged. Fortunately, regional powers have recognized these emerging threats; in January 2004, an Association of South East Asian Nations (ASEAN) meeting was held to discuss fighting transnational crimes and terrorism.

13

Colombia: A Sophisticated, Transnational Narco-State

Just to the south of the United States lies the "country" of *FARCLANDIA*. This term is widely used to define the area controlled by the Revolutionary Armed Forces of Colombia, or FARC. FARC was established in 1966 as a communist insurgency group with the goal of overthrowing the Colombian government. As the revenue from the drug trade expanded, so has the power and influence of FARC, which now controls an estimated 40 percent of Colombia through a negotiated agreement with the government. This area includes FARC's "safe haven," which is used for the cultivation of narcotics and as training and staging grounds for assaults on the Colombian military. Experts estimate that FARC's illegal activities net $200–400 million annually, one-half from drug cultivation and trafficking, with the remainder coming from kidnapping, extortion, and other criminal activities.[18]

FARC—by the nature of its business—is a regional transnational criminal organization. However, the government is concerned with FARC's global transnational activities, including increased cooperation with the Russian mafia, a relationship cultivated over the last decade. In the late 1990s, the Russians built an arms pipeline to Colombia, bringing in thousands of weapons and tons of other supplies to help FARC fight their war against the Colombian government. In return the planes were loaded with 40,000 kilograms of cocaine that the Russian mafia then distributed for profit. The liaison between these two entities is increasingly troublesome, as Russian organized crime flourishes and government corruption grows. FARC is now linked to a Tijuana, Mexico, cartel; the State Department believes they supplied cocaine to the Tijuana cartel in return for cash and weapons. Authorities believe that FARC is now extending its cooperation to the borders of the United States.[19] FARC is a perfect example of a growing transnational threat that evolved from being state-sponsored to sponsoring the state to becoming its own entity.

Emerging Area of Concern: North Korea

A region worth watching is the area surrounding North Korea. Unlike other cases discussed where organized crime attempts to infiltrate a country and its government, the government of North Korea is infiltrating organized crime.

As the economy continues to decline, the government of North Korea turned to drug trafficking (methamphetamines, opium, and heroin), human trafficking, and organized crime for funding. According to experts, members of the armed forces, the diplomatic corps, and the intelligence service are engaging in narcotics trafficking, and there is evidence of printing plants being used to produce high-quality counterfeit currency. There are also indicators that North Korean crime is set to expand beyond the nation's borders, thus becoming a transnational threat in the region. Japan expressed concern that members of its local Korean population have ties to North Korea's organized crime factions.[20]

Fighting Transnational Crime

In December 2000, UN Secretary-General Kofi Annan stated:

> If crime crosses all borders, so must law enforcement. If the rule of law is undermined not only in one country, but also in many, then those who defend it cannot limit themselves to purely national means. If the enemies of progress and human rights seek to exploit the openness and opportunities of globalization for their purposes, then we must exploit those very same factors to defend human rights, and defeat the forces of crime, corruption, and trafficking in human beings.[21]

Our national strategy of international engagement to fight transnational crime falls directly in line with Mr. Annan's prescient guidance.

The burden of squelching government corruption, establishing and enforcing the rule of law, and fighting crime lies with the affected countries. However, much of this transnational criminal activity is spreading to the United States. With the emerging possibility of terrorist ties, our government stepped up engagement with other nations to address the problem. To most effectively confront international crime, we must pursue international laws and programs. US agencies are working to help nations identify loopholes in their laws, strengthen borders, and build capacity to deal with the expanding transnational crime epidemic. According to Schrage, "Targeted intelligence and operations may remove specific terrorist, drug trafficking, or organized crime groups, but unless we address the environments that allow them to thrive, we will have at best created a void that can be filled by others."[22] To understand how our government is battling transnational crime, it is imperative to review agencies, methods, progress, and lessons learned.

Agencies and Methods

According to the State Department, INL is responsible for the development of policies and the management of more than $1 billion in programs globally to combat transnational criminal threats and strengthen the rule of law and relevant institutions in emerging democracies. INL programs support two of the State Department's strategic goals: to reduce the entry of illegal drugs into the United States and to minimize the impact of international crime on the United States and its citizens.[23]

It is important to understand that each government agency possesses different statutory responsibilities, specialized skill sets, and unique "culture." The State Department is in the diplomacy and relationship-building business; thus, INL is involved in myriad training, negotiating, and coordinating activities. Areas of focus include counternarcotics, demand reduction, money laundering, financial crime, terrorist financing, smuggling of goods, illegal migration, trafficking in persons, domestic violence, border controls, document security, corruption, cyber crime, intellectual property rights, law enforcement, police academy development, and assistance to judiciaries and prosecutors. This work crosses into the jurisdiction of many other government agencies and is accomplished with the help of investigators (FBI), prosecutors (Department of Justice [DOJ]), money experts (Department of Treasury), intelligence gatherers (Central Intelligence Agency [CIA]), and myriad other US agencies.

Under the umbrella of INL's program, DOJ worked extensively to develop foreign law-enforcement institutions, to build the rule of law, and provide resident legal advisors to countries to give them on-the-ground advice in how to establish appropriate legal institutions for domestic security and to help confront transnational threats. INL established International Law Enforcement

16

Academies (ILEA). The ILEA program is an interagency effort with 16 US law-enforcement agencies participating. Serving as a global model for advancing our common fight against international crime and promoting the rule of law, they build relationships between law-enforcement officials, support democracy in policing operations, and raise the professionalism of officers involved in the fight against crime. The focus of instruction is not just technical in nature but, more importantly, includes the development of leadership and management skills to deal with the modern challenges facing law enforcement.

The DOJ's Office of Overseas Prosecutorial Development, Assistance, and Training (OPDAT) specifically focuses on organized crime. It gives prosecutors and investigators specialized tools and familiarization with unique aspects of pursuing organized crime. OPDAT provides a money-laundering seminar that is designed to familiarize law-enforcement personnel, policy makers, and legislators with international standards. It also involves developing and using legislation, investigative techniques, and prosecutorial tools in fighting money laundering, bank fraud, terrorist financing, and other complex financial crimes.[24]

Another tool, Mutual Legal Assistance Treaties (MLAT), leverages our ability to fight transnational crime. An MLAT allows US authorities to obtain evidence and other types of law-enforcement assistance from other countries. Foreign governments can use the MLAT to request assistance from the United States. This tool greatly helps when pursuing and extraditing international criminals and is effective in the pursuit of terrorists and their supporters.

The Lyon Group, chaired by INL and formed in 1995 by the G-7/8, is effective in coordinating efforts to fight international crime. The group made great progress in setting international standards and enhancing law-enforcement cooperation against transnational crime and terrorism, including identifying and removing obstacles to cooperation and facilitating information sharing.[25] Other US law-enforcement agencies actively support INL's efforts. For instance, the FBI's Eurasian Organized Crime Unit was established to reduce the threat to American society posed by related crime; they work extensively with the law-enforcement subgroup of the G-7/8.

Progress and Lessons Learned

The State Department highlights three areas of major progress in the battle against transnational crime: trafficking in persons, money laundering, and counternarcotics. These global crimes, linked with organized crime, continue to impact the United States and have the potential to be accessed or used as models by terrorist groups.

Trafficking in Persons. The State Department estimates that 800,000 to 900,000 men, women, and children are trafficked every year.[26] This crime violates basic human rights, introduces serious public health risks, and, unfortunately, fuels organized crime. Although many countries look the other way, the United States is directly confronting this form of modern-day slavery and through direct engagement encourages others to do the same.

State Department efforts focus on prevention of trafficking, protection of victims (and potential victims), and criminal prosecution. The United States provided assistance to Russia when drafting its aggressive antitrafficking legislation to criminalize human trafficking to provide protection for victims and witnesses in human-trafficking cases and mandate government-funded public awareness campaigns. Ukraine is another large-source country for trafficking victims to all parts of Europe and around the globe and has a comprehensive action plan for each government ministry to support public awareness, education, and prosecution. The State Department regularly issues human-trafficking reports, ranking countries by tiers and highlighting their individual trafficking problem. The global distribution of this report pressured governments to comply. In the United States, the Trafficking Victims Protection Act enforces the rule of law and allows global pursuit of traffickers.

Money Laundering. Money laundering is an activity that goes hand-in-hand with most profit-generating criminal activities. The individual or group has "dirty money" and must find an opaque way to hide, move, or transform it to protect operations. Killing sources and identifying methods of money laundering can help eliminate criminal activity, and tracing the money often reveals other criminal operations.

The Financial Action Task Force on Money Laundering (FATF) is an intergovernmental body of 31 member countries. FATF's purpose is to develop and promote policies at national and international levels and to combat money laundering and terrorist financing.[27] Through participation in the FATF, INL plays an important role in formulating global anti-money-laundering training, programs, and policies. INL also funds and participates in the Council of Europe's anti-money-laundering organization, MoneyVal, which is comprised of 24 member states. MoneyVal is a forum to discuss the implementation of international money-laundering standards and to evaluate effectiveness in implementation.

Russia made substantial strides in combating money laundering in the last few years. On 1 February 2002 Russia's new financial investigation unit, the Financial Monitoring Committee, began collecting suspicious activity reports from banks and coordinating all of Russia's anti-money-laundering and counterterrorist financing efforts. In 2002 Russia was removed from the FATF Non-Cooperative Countries and Territories list and was admitted to FATF in 2003.

The US government also engages with Ukraine regarding their sizable money-laundering issues through FATF. In September 2001 FATF placed Ukraine on its Non-Cooperative Countries and Territories list, citing inadequacies in Ukraine's anti-money-laundering regime. In November 2002 Ukraine passed a comprehensive anti-money-laundering law, but FATF is still reviewing Ukraine's efforts for possible removal from the Non-Cooperative Countries and Territories list.

Counternarcotics. The US government continues to expend resources fighting the global drug cultivation and trafficking epidemic on many fronts. The flow of Afghan heroin into and across Russia has increased tremendously with the size of heroin seizures increasing to an average of 50 to 60 kilograms—this despite Russia being party to the 1988 UN Drug Convention and other UN agreements to combat drug trafficking. Russia appears to be on the offensive in the war on drugs. In 1998 the Russian government enacted the Law on Narcotics and Psychotropic Substances, criminalizing the purchase and possession of drugs and increasing trafficking penalties. In March 2003 Russian president Vladimir V. Putin transferred responsibility for the investigation of narcotics trafficking from the Ministry of Internal Affairs to the newly formed State Committee for the Control of Narcotics and Psychotropic Substances (GKN). There are also signs of new cooperation between Russian law enforcement and a new counternarcotics Special Investigative Unit created and vetted by the Drug Enforcement Administration (DEA) in Uzbekistan. The United States and Russia signed the first bilateral agreement on law-enforcement assistance, with the United States providing more than $4 million for training and equipment to Russian units fighting drug trafficking along Russia's southern border with Kazakhstan and for training and equipment to improve narcotics searches and seizures at important ports in the northwest and south of Russia.

The Ukrainian government is working to address its poppy and hemp cultivation issues. Ukraine is also party to the 1988 UN Drug Convention. Although narcotics trafficking continues to be a national priority for law-enforcement bodies, lack of financial resources and interagency cooperation as well as weak regulatory constraints seriously hinder the government's efforts. The United States is providing assistance and hopes to use any Ukrainian progress as a model for other similarly challenged countries in the region.

The Balkans is an area of great success in relation to law enforcement and, ultimately, drug abatement. INL funded a DOJ project to train Albanian police and prosecutors in modern investigative and prosecutorial techniques. It focused on disrupting and dismantling organized criminal enterprises and on enhancing the capabilities of the prosecution service and on establishing international standards of border security at three major ports of entry.[28] Through this effort, they hope to significantly reduce the amount of drugs crossing Albanian borders.

Corruption. A corrupt government is one that is susceptible to organized crime and potentially to terrorists. INL plays a major role in efforts to assist countries in combating corruption. In 1994 the European Ministers of Justice considered corruption to be a serious threat to democracy, to the rule of law, and to human rights. Several annual conferences were held on the subject. In response to growing corruption in the region, the Council of Europe's Group of States Against Corruption (GRECO) was established in 1999. Members include 37 European countries and the United States. GRECO provides a forum to discuss and evaluate anticorruption efforts of member states. Along with helping countries establish and enforce the rule of law, the formation of regional groups such as GRECO is another type of capacity building that will fortify nations and help repel corruption.

Lessons Learned

The State Department's lessons learned while combating transnational crime, as related by Schrage to the Senate, could easily be applied to the new global war on terror. The lessons are of importance for policy makers.

1. Fighting transnational crime takes regional and international cooperation. Promoting the rule of law and fostering international law-enforcement cooperation is a preeminent objective of US foreign policy and of the international community of nations. The rule of law and effective law enforcement form a foundation on which commerce and investment, economic development, and respect for human rights can be built. This nation-building activity will also prevent corruption, which fuels organized crime.

2. Interagency coordination is important. The United States provides an excellent model to the world by drawing from the strengths of our various government agencies to fight crime at home. The State Department asserts that the most progress is seen in countries when the various strengths of different agencies can be brought to bear as part of a unified strategy, with a strong recognition and respect for the great expertise shared by US law-enforcement officials.

3. A project-based approach to programs focused on integrated country strategies is critical. INL moved aggressively to institute a project-based approach to programs, signing letters of agreement with host governments that detail not only the various projects and funding levels in assistance programs but also the obligations of the host

21

government. This activity reinforces that fighting transnational crime is a shared fight, using shared resources and having shared responsibility.

4. Linking country strategies to crosscutting international strategies is essential. In confronting transnational threats, efforts in different bilateral programs are coordinated so that they are focused on areas that will have the greatest impact in promoting US objectives.[29] For instance, methods of engagement may depend on the type of actor, such as a former enemy, a rogue state, or an unwilling participant. In this sense, country or regional strategies to battle transnational crime must be coordinated with US overarching goals and objectives.

Despite the resources expended by the United States and countries around the world, transnational organized crime and terrorist groups are thriving. Is there a connection?

Notes

1. Ashley, "Transnational Organized Crime."
2. Global Business Consulting Incorporated's (GBCI) Official Web site.
3. Ashley, "Transnational Organized Crime."
4. General Accounting Office (GAO), "Combating Terrorism."
5. Pifer, "Combating Transnational Crime and Corruption in Europe."
6. Schrage, "Combating Transnational Crime and Corruption in Europe."
7. Department of State, "Victims of Trafficking and Violence Protection Act of 2000."
8. Cilluffo, "The Threat Posed from the Convergence of Organized Crime, Drug Trafficking, and Terrorism."
9. Ashley, "Transnational Organized Crime."
10. Schrage, "Combating Transnational Crime and Corruption in Europe."
11. GAO, "Combating Terrorism."
12. Cilluffo, "The Threat Posed from the Convergence of Organized Crime, Drug Trafficking, and Terrorism."
13. Schrage, "Combating Transnational Crime and Corruption in Europe."
14. Ashley, "Transnational Organized Crime."
15. Asian-Nation, The Landscape of Asian America, "Asian-American Gangs."
16. Ibid.
17. GAO, "Combating Terrorism."
18. Council on Foreign Relations, "Are There Terrorists in Colombia?"

19. Cilluffo, "The Threat Posed from the Convergence of Organized Crime, Drug Trafficking, and Terrorism."

20. Ibid.

21. Annan, "U.N. Statement on Convention against Organized Crime."

22. Schrage, "Combating Transnational Crime and Corruption in Europe."

23. Department of State. "Bureau for International Narcotics and Law Enforcement Affairs."

24. Schrage, "Combating Transnational Crime and Corruption in Europe."

25. Ibid.

26. Department of State, "Trafficking in Persons Report."

27. Financial Action Task Force on Money Laundering, "What Is Money Laundering?"

28. Schrage, "Combating Transnational Crime and Corruption in Europe."

29. Ibid.

Chapter 3

The Criminal-Terrorist Nexus: Funding Terror

The growing nexus between terrorists, narcotics traffickers, and other international criminals that has been fostered by developments in international communications, travel and information-sharing, and the end of the Cold War.

—Pres. William J. "Bill" Clinton
1995 Address to the UN

President Clinton's above statement is one of the first public references to an emerging nexus between international criminals and terrorists. The word *nexus* is derived from the Latin word *nectere*, which is also the source of the English word *connect*; therefore, the criminal-terrorist nexus is the connection between criminal activity and terrorism.

The intersection of these lethal activities can be in the form of imitation of operational tactics or in the sharing of resources. Similar to transnational organized crime groups, terrorist organizations are benefiting from transnational operations and access to advanced technologies that provide them with greater destructive power, greater ease of movement and concealment, and the means to spread their message globally.[1] Frank J. Cilluffo, an expert on the nexus, testified to Congress in 2000 that "the lines between organized crime, drug trafficking, and terrorism are quickly becoming blurred."[2] Many experts agree. They add that as a terrorist group reaches a certain point in development, it can easily turn into a criminal group. The Abu Sayyaf Group's exploitation of marijuana plantations in the Philippines is commonly used as an example.[3] As we close down other routes of financing and pursue groups globally, terrorist cells may have no alternative to organized crime. And as with other transnational organized crime groups, the cells operate with the sophistication of multinational corporations to generate an unbelievable amount of resources.

Funding Terror

Richard A. Clarke, former terrorism coordinator for the National Security Council, testified in 2003: "When I first asked the CIA in 1995, in that era, to look into terrorist financing, they said: 'well, after all, you have to understand it doesn't take a lot of money to do a terrorist act.' What they failed to understand was that it took a lot of money to be a terrorist organization."[4] An old soldier's axiom provides excellent context to the importance of pursuing terror financing: "Amateurs study tactics, professionals study logistics." This study argues that the money trail is the key to unraveling future operations, more so than any other aspect of terrorism investigative work.

Terrorist organizations need money and resources not only to carry out an operation but perhaps most importantly to recruit, maintain safe havens, train, travel, take care of day-to-day expenses, and, in some groups, provide for the families of dead martyrs. The assets required to fund such extensive, global operations synonymous with modern terrorist groups come from a variety of licit and illicit sources—individuals, organizations, and the criminal enterprise. One widely used estimate is that economic activity related to terrorism accounts for a staggering $1.5 trillion, or 5 percent, of annual global output.[5] After a 10-year period, al-Qaeda was estimated to receive between $300 million and $500 million in cash, averaging $30 to $50 million a year.[6] Approximately 10 percent of spending was allocated to operations, while 90 percent was used to maintain the infrastructure of the network, including payments to other groups to support them or to increase al-Qaeda's influence in these regions.[7] Much was discussed in the media about the mere $450,000 that was required to finance 9/11 terrorist attacks; this discussion led to a false impression in the public and among many policy makers that the money trail is not sizeable, worrisome, or integral to a terrorist operation. That is faulty logic. In fact, the cost of doing business may be rising for terrorists; similar to a business that expands into franchises, splinter groups need resources to sustain themselves, which drives the cost of doing business higher. This requirement may lead them to previously untapped sources for money, manpower, and other support.

The GAO differentiates between methods terrorist groups employ to earn, move, and store assets.[8] Although some terrorist fund-raising activities are involved in more than one aspect of resource management, this model is helpful when applied to transnational organized crime.

Terrorists earn money through a variety of activities. Donations from wealthy supporters and personal wealth of those involved in the group are two of the "cleanest" sources. They are not business activities and are thus untraceable, impermeable ways to generate funds. International charities and use of tithing by religious believers is the next desirable activity as well as mixing illicit and licit funds to complicate the money trail. When necessary, terrorist groups move on to other activities such as involvement in illegal drug trade, commodity smuggling such as cigarettes, and identity theft and fraud.

Terrorists move assets either by laundering, concealing (smuggling or using "hawala"), or conversion to internationally traded commodities. The methods employed seek nontransparent systems in which they are able to hide transactions and movement across borders. Legitimate systems are sometimes used, although the means of movement will be illicit in nature. Financial transactions may also be layered, which provides additional protection to the movement. The sophistication and international aspect of such activity has long been underestimated; one expert believes that terrorist organizations have shown the same skills as any Wall Street investor in channeling assets into legal structures and businesses in pursuit of their broader goals.[9]

Terrorists may store assets in commodities that maintain or increase in value over time such as diamonds or gold. Precious metals and stones are regarded as currency in many parts of the world and are relatively easy to smuggle and are untraceable. Bulk cash can also be considered such a commodity.

International Charities and "Zakat"

The use of charities to raise funds for terrorist groups is widely covered in the media and is the focal effort of several government agencies. Modern charities are global in nature, and many are the equivalent of large-scale corporations. The use of charities to raise funds is desirable primarily because of the ability to commingle illicit funds with licit funds. Also, deliberate contributors wishing to finance the terrorist group are protected due to lack of paper trail and the commingling of funds. The process of designating a charity as a source of terrorist funding is complex and lengthy; the burden of proof is extensive, and upon designation all funds are frozen as it is impossible to separate the "good" money from the "bad." However, despite the nontransparency inherent in charitable giving, governments are making progress in identifying and closing off this source of terrorist financing.

Since the 9/11 attacks, the United States and other governments working to staunch the flow of money to terrorist groups have frozen more than $136 million in monetary assets they claim assisted al-Qaeda or other terrorist groups. This action includes 1,439 blocked accounts.[10] However, it is very important that this data be scrutinized and fully understood before declaring a victory; since licit funds are intermingled with illicit funds, it is unknown how much money was withheld from terrorists.

In 2003 the Treasury Department revoked the tax-exempt status of three Muslim charities that the US government has accused of diverting contributions to help bankroll terrorist activities: Benevolence International Foundation of Palos Hills, Illinois; the Holy Land Foundation for Relief and Development of Richardson, Texas; and the Global Relief Foundation of Bridgeview, Illinois. The three charities were "designated" under presidential Executive Order 13324, meaning that financial assets and incoming donations were frozen. Also, their tax-exempt status was revoked, so donors cannot deduct any contributions made to the group, and the organization must pay federal income tax.[11] Enaam Arnaout, who ran Benevolence International Foundation, plead guilty to aiding Islamic fighters in Chechnya. His operation had offices worldwide, which allowed it to easily move and hide assets.[12] The Holy Land Foundation, which the administration said raised $13 million in 2000, is the largest Muslim charity in the United States. Although claiming that donations went to aid Palestinians, it was singled out for its alleged support of Harakat Al-

Muqawama Al-Islamia (HAMAS), the Islamic Resistance Movement, mainly to support the families of bombers.[13] The Global Relief Fund, another multimillion-dollar business, sent more than 90 percent of donations overseas and at the very least, lied to the US government about the scope and destination of those funds.[14] Court filings and testimony regarding designated charities provide a good education on the difficulties unraveling the paper trail, identifying licit from illicit funds, and determining legal and illegal recipients of the money.

On 22 January 2004, the United States and Saudi Arabia jointly announced the addition of four branches of the Al-Haramain Islamic Foundation to its consolidated list of terrorists connected to al-Qaeda. According to the Treasury Department, in 2003 the Saudi government ordered Al-Haramain to close all of its overseas branches. However, they continued to operate; the branch in Bosnia-Herzegovina was simply renamed 'Vazir' and continued business.[15] This example illustrates the ease of designated charities to reorganize, evade authorities, and continue fund-raising.

The US government also may target individual "businessmen" for their charity-related dealings. The case of Abdurahman Alamoudi, a very popular and charismatic Muslim imam who faced several felony convictions, has received much publicity. Alamoudi was born in Ethiopian-occupied Eritrea and immigrated to the United States in 1979 and in 1996 become a naturalized US citizen. He holds a Yemeni passport and is allied with the group, Muslim Brotherhood. While visiting in London in 2003, Alamoudi received $340,000 in cash from a Libyan. A few days later, officials at London's Heathrow Airport detained him with the cash as he attempted to board a flight to Syria. During his detention with British authorities, Alamoudi said specifically that he intended to launder the Libyan money back into the United States through Saudi banks. He intended to deposit the money in banks located in Saudi Arabia from where he would feed it back in smaller sums into accounts in the United States. US law sets no limits on cash entering the country, but the law requires the bearer to report amounts of $10,000 or more via customs declaration forms, thus forcing Alamoudi to devise a plan for transferring the money in smaller sums.

29

British authorities allowed him to return to the United States, and he was subsequently arrested at Dulles International Airport on 29 September 2003. Alamoudi lied on his US customs form, notably leaving out his travels to Libya, Lebanon, Yemen, and Egypt. He was charged with the following federal offenses: illegal transactions with a terrorist regime, passport fraud, conspiracy to fund terrorists directed against US forces in Iraq, and material support for terrorists in the United States. Alamoudi was sentenced on 15 October 2004 to the maximum penalty of 23 years in prison after pleading guilty to immigration fraud and illegal business dealings with Libya. What was the explanation for his actions? Since the Libyan regime had by then renounced terrorism, he felt obliged to "bridge the gulf" between his adopted country and an Islamic state.[16]

Alamoudi ran, directed, founded, or funded at least 15 Muslim political-action and charitable groups that represented the public voice of Islamic Americans. The FBI submitted evidence showing that Alamoudi's American Muslim Foundation (AMF), a charitable offshoot of his American Muslim Council (AMC), funded two suspected terrorists in Oregon who were arrested in 2003. Also worrisome is Alamoudi's involvement with the certification of Muslim chaplains for the Department of Defense. Notably, through AMC, he spun off the American Muslim Armed Forces and Veterans Affairs Council, one of three Islamic organizations to certify chaplains for the military. Alamoudi has political savvy; he and a group of Muslim leaders met with Pres. George W. Bush in Austin, Texas, in July 2002. Alamoudi's case is disturbing, particularly when his power, connections, and possible motives are taken into account.

The case of the al Taqwa financial empire—which operated in the Middle East, Turkey, Italy, Switzerland, Lichtenstein, and the Bahamas—underscores the difficulty of disrupting the shadowy world of terrorist financing without strong international assistance. US investigators believe that al Taqwa, which means "Fear of God," funneled tens of millions of dollars to al-Qaeda, HAMAS, and other terrorist groups through charities and informal banking arrangements. The two central figures in al Taqwa, who live abroad, were placed on an international list of terrorist financiers, which requires member nations to seize their assets and ban them from traveling internationally. However, a UN Security Council committee report notes that both are evading the spirit of antiterrorism sanctions against them by traveling and continuing to operate a hotel and several pieces of real estate.[17] Unfortunately, there is no formal mechanism to reprimand countries that do not assist with the enforcement of sanctions or reward them for their efforts.

Designation of a charity is an action that can lead to a loss of goodwill and can damage US relationships with countries that legitimately receive aid, which is probably why the State Department is heavily involved in the process. For example, among the accounts blocked since 9/11 are 23 belonging to Islamic charities that collect and donate money for medical, educational, housing, and other needs to impoverished Muslims in the Middle East and elsewhere. However, US law-enforcement agencies contend that all 23 are fronts for financing terrorist organizations and all assets remain frozen.[18]

Zakat, or charitable giving, is another fundraising mechanism that received far less attention but might be of more significance. A little-known report prepared by French financing expert Jean-Charles Brisard for the UN Security Council entitled *Terrorism Financing: Roots and Trends of Saudi Terrorism Financing*, provides the most insight into this complex cultural issue. Brisard believes that *zakat* is the most important source of terrorism funding and that most of it is moved through the legal banking system. *Zakat* is charitable giving that is part of every devout Muslim's obligations and usually peaks during the season of Ramadan. According to his estimate, Saudis contribute approximately $10 billion per year in *zakat* donations, which then usually take the form of bank transfers to approximately 240 charities. The lack of bookkeeping for *zakat* and other charitable giving makes intervening difficult, and countries are extremely sensitive about monitoring religious giving. It was widely publicized when Saudi authorities began to remove "collection boxes" outside of their mosques and businesses, but the amount of money collected in those boxes represented only $60,000 a year.[19] This amount pales in comparison to the amount donated through *zakat*, a system that certainly requires more scrutiny by our international partners in the fight against terrorist funding.

Narco-Terror

Immediately after the terrorist attacks on 9/11, President Bush stated that "it is so important for Americans to know that the traffic in drugs finances the work of terror, sustaining terrorists, that terrorists use drug profits to fund their cells to commit acts of murder. If you quit drugs, you join the fight against terror in America."[20] The DEA used his words, along with a unique television advertising campaign to alert US citizens that their illegal drug use may be directly connected to terrorism. Although the campaign is over, this important message must be driven home: drug cultivation, trafficking, and use are a threat to our national security.

Narco-terrorism is a worldwide threat. It knows no ideological or traditional territorial boundaries. Groups from the far right to the far left and every group in between are susceptible to the lure of drug money. The vast majority of major terrorist organizations relies, at least in part, on the drug trade as a source funding.[21] A decline in state-sponsorship of terrorism, one of the major diplomatic goals of the US government, may further drive terrorists into the drug trade. Whether terrorists actively cultivate and traffic drugs or "tax" those who do, the financial windfall that the narcotics industry guarantees filled the void left by state sponsors.[22] The terrorist and criminal drug industry continues to thrive globally, despite most nation-states reporting that they are fundamentally opposed to its existence on their soil.

Terrorists and drug traffickers have a symbiotic association. According to the DEA, terror and drug groups are linked in this mutually beneficial relationship by money, tactics, geography, and politics. Drug traffickers and terrorists use similar methods to achieve their criminal ends. Most important, they share a common disregard for human life. Many drug-trafficking organizations engage in acts that most people would consider terrorist in nature, such as the public killing of innocents, large-scale bombings intended to intimidate governments, kidnappings, and tortures.[23] Although one might believe that religious fundamentalists would not involve themselves with criminals such as drug traffickers, consider the quote by Muslim radical Abu-Hamza Al-Masri when discussing the use of nuclear war to defend Muslims: "Islam permits it, as it permits a man to eat pork if he is starving."[24] Moral righteousness is thus situational and is applied when it best serves the needs of the terrorists.

According to Cilluffo, drug traffickers and terrorist organizations attack the underpinnings of legitimate government institutions to achieve their objectives, or they enjoy the protection of governments that condone terror or drug trafficking. Drug traffickers and terror groups are drawn to regions where central government authority is weak. If a terror group already controls a region and has excluded or neutralized legitimate government institutions, drug production only requires a business deal.[25] Drug trafficking is particularly alluring to terrorists; organized crime groups run the overall business operations, while the terrorists collect enormous taxes along the distribution route. For example, the Taliban gets funding from taxing all aspects of the drug trade. Opium harvests are taxed at around 12 percent, and heroin-manufacturing labs are taxed at $70 per kilogram of heroin. In the final stage, the Taliban gives transporters a permit for $250 per kilo of heroin to carry for presentation to Taliban checkpoints throughout the country. The *Observatoire Geopolitique des Drogues* estimates that this adds up to $75 million per year in taxes for the Taliban.[26] The Taliban was a major source of funding for al-Qaeda in Afghanistan prior to US operations.

However, al-Qaeda continues to traffic drugs, with or without the support of the Taliban. The extent of al-Qaeda's ongoing drug operations was realized in December 2003, when the US Navy seized three al-Qaeda-linked boats. In the first operation in the Persian Gulf near the Strait of Hormuz, a Navy destroyer stopped a 40-foot boat, arrested three men, and confiscated two tons of hashish worth $10 million. A day after the announcement, Navy ships on interdiction duty in the Arabian Sea captured two sailboats carrying 85 pounds of heroin valued at $3 million. The crew was suspected of links to al-Qaeda. The Navy also found 150 pounds of methamphetamines worth $1.5 million. A Department of Defense official said all the drugs likely came from Afghanistan.[27]

Many believe that a business model for al-Qaeda's drug-trafficking quest is FARC. It is self-contained and has no need for financial allies or state-sponsorship. Afghanistan and Colombia command the market share of the opiate and co-

caine production in the world, and as one expert stated, they
are the "blue chips of the narcotics industry."[28] An area of
deep concern for al-Qaeda experts is the potential or existing
relationship between these two cartels. Two days before 9/11,
the DEA seized 53 kilograms of Afghan heroin in New York. It
was being distributed by Colombians.[29]

Pharmaceutical sales in the United States may be the next
drug-related frontier for terrorists, who have possibly already
used them to funnel money to Middle Eastern terrorist groups,
including Hezbollah. Four Detroit men with ties to Jordan,
Yemen, Lebanon, and other Middle Eastern countries smuggled
pseudoephedrine from Canada to locations in the Midwest—
primarily Detroit and Chicago. Pseudoephedrine, which is used
in cold and allergy medications, is an essential ingredient in
methamphetamine, a powerful and popular drug also known as
ice or crystal meth. The chemical was sold to Mexican-run
methamphetamine operations in the western United States with
some of the proceeds of the resulting drug sales diverted to Middle East accounts linked to terrorist groups. The drug ring was
broken up on 10 January 2002 as part of a massive DEA investigation called Operation Mountain Express.[30] DEA agents told
the author that although seizures of this amount are fairly rou-
tine, the connection to an international terrorist group was unexpected and extremely worrisome.

International drug-trafficking rings are certainly multinational corporations and exhibit all of the same characteristics.
They may exhibit some of the same weaknesses; these must be
identified and exploited to unravel the enormous narco-terror
syndicate.

Commodities Smuggling

Unlike other methods employed by terrorists, commodities
smuggling is not about moving money, but value. For instance,
a multimillion-dollar interstate cigarette-smuggling ring contributed some of its proceeds to the terrorist organization
Hezbollah. Twelve people were indicted in this scheme for purchasing low-tax cigarettes in North Carolina (5-cents tax per
pack) and reselling them in Michigan (75-cents tax per pack),
which caused at least a $2 million tax loss for the state of Michi-

gan between 1997 and 1999. The leader stated some of the proceeds were to Hezbollah for the "orphans of martyrs" program to benefit the families of those killed in the group's operations or by Hezbollah's enemies.[31] This case is a perfect example of the market savvy exhibited by terrorist groups: focus on the highest possible profit margin and move a product with high, consistent demand. Similar commodities are at risk and bear watching.

Identity Theft and Fraud

The sophisticated white-collar crimes of identity theft and credit-card fraud are no longer just a consumer issue. When federal investigators unraveled the 9/11 money trail, it suddenly became an issue related to global terrorism. The hijackers used phony identification (ID), Social Security numbers, and birth dates to establish bank accounts and create their lives in the United States. Landlords, flight schools, banks, and other institutions fell prey. Seven of the hijackers obtained ID cards through the Virginia Department of Motor Vehicles (DMV) even though none lived in the state. They took advantage of rules allowing individuals to meet residency requirements with a simple notarized letter, a system long abused by immigrants, immigration lawyers, and local notaries. Despite previous warnings from the FBI and DMV investigators, the department maintained the system.[32]

Identity crimes and related credit-card fraud also can be a source of terrorist fund-raising. In its simplest form, the theft of a credit card enables the criminal to purchase goods (often for resale) or withdraw money, at least until the theft is detected and the owner cancels the card. Credit applications abound, and it is simple for criminals to open multiple accounts in the name of other individuals or an alias, and then simply disappear before being caught. In more complex schemes, bogus credit cards are manufactured, distributed, and used by the terrorists. However, transactions made with a stolen or manufactured credit card leave the unappealing paper trail and images captured on video cameras. More attractive because of its nontransparency and ability to access a subject's credit for a longer period is a growing criminal act called "skimming," a tactic employed by a master counterfeiter and terrorist supporter Youssef Hmimssa.

35

Hmimssa was arrested immediately after 9/11 when he was caught furnishing fake visas and other ID credentials to a suspected terrorist cell in Detroit. His apartment yielded documents including a day planner that the government says contained sketches of a US air base in Turkey and a videotape of potential future terrorist targets in Los Angeles, New York, and other locations. He confessed his crimes in the public arena to explain how easy identity theft and fraud is to perpetrate, and in 2003 he was summoned to testify to the Senate Finance Committee to enlighten lawmakers. His testimony is riveting and troubling. In support of his efforts, Hmimssa recruited a fellow Moroccan—a taxi driver and waiter at a north suburban restaurant—to steal customers' credit card numbers. He provided his codefendant with a pocket-sized device with a scanning slot, which resembles a pager. With a single swipe, the skimming device copies encoded information on the card's magnetic strip. The driver/waiter swiped diners' credit cards through the device and then gave the skimmer to Hmimssa, who downloaded the information using a laptop computer. The pair skimmed about 250 credit card account numbers and bilked customers of more than $100,000.

Identity theft and related crimes have been detected in many terrorist cells in the last five years. Ahmed Ressam, a member the Armed Islamic Group (with ties to Osama bin Laden), was caught in December 1999 at the US-Canadian border with 100 pounds of explosives stashed in the wheel bed of the trunk of his rental car. He had assumed the name Benni Norris, which he used to open bank accounts and obtain a passport, a false birth certificate, and a student ID. He told authorities that he relied on welfare and petty crime, including credit-card fraud and trafficking in identity documents, for financial support. He was linked to a theft ring suspected stealing more than 5,000 items, including computers, cellular phones, passports, and credit cards, with the goal of financing Muslim extremist groups.[33] In his so-called millennium plot, Ressam planned to set off an explosion at the Los Angeles International Airport. Others involved with the operation told FBI agents they supported themselves through credit-card fraud and used proceeds from that scam and others to finance their mission. They used countless stolen and fraudulent identities, including 13 stolen by an accomplice from the membership computer of a Bally's fitness club in Boston. They also had plans to buy a gas station and use that as an avenue to secretly obtain credit-card numbers, placing a camera in a location where it would be possible to watch people punching in their personal identification numbers.

Al-Qaeda uses credit-card scams and identity theft extensively. The 9/11 hijackers had a scheme in Spain to raise money for the attacks, and according to authorities, "The pattern was very clear within the North African contingent of al-Qaeda members operating in Europe. Every time you arrest one of them he has 20 different identities and 20 different credit cards." Other suspected terrorist cells operating in the United States, Canada, and Europe have employed a variety of scams to steal millions of dollars from credit card companies. At a 2001 Senate hearing, the former deputy assistant director of the Secret Service gave senators a glimpse of two groups of Middle Easterners with ties to terrorist groups who allegedly were involved in massive credit card fraud in the United States, bilking financial institutions of $21 million. Dennis Lormel, chief of the FBI's Financial Crimes Section, told the House Financial Services Committee that "the ease with which these individuals can obtain false identification or assume the identity of someone else, and then open bank accounts and obtain credit cards, makes these attractive ways to generate funds."[34]

According to federal agents, an emerging area of concern related to credit cards is often referred to by law enforcement as a "bust-out" scam, involving the use of credit card "courtesy checks." Often, attached to the monthly credit card statement are several checks that can be used by the consumer in any fashion, with charges going against the credit card. The checks are widely accepted, so with just one extra piece of fabricated identification, the criminal can use all three checks in short order, even exceeding the consumer's line of credit. A bust-out scam was uncovered in 2001 when two groups of Middle Easterners with extensive affiliations to known Islamic terrorist organizations were arrested for various identity theft and fraud crimes.[35]

The links between terrorists and sophisticated white-collar crimes such as identity theft and related fraud is irrefutable.

Technological advances have only made this crime easier to commit, and it remains a lucrative means of raising funds for terrorist groups.

Money Laundering

Money laundering is the practice of engaging in financial transactions to conceal the identities, sources, and destinations of the money in question.[36] Traditional money laundering makes "dirty" money "clean" after the crime was committed. Criminal money laundering is as simple as putting a dirty one-dollar bill into a vending machine, hitting "change return" and getting four clean quarters. Casinos are vulnerable to money laundering; the patron exchanges the dirty money for chips and then cashes out. Laundering can be as complex as washing money through an international corporation or a chain of businesses. The crime is committed, and the resulting money must be dealt with.

However, terrorist-related money laundering is a far different activity. The crime (terrorist operation) has not yet occurred. The money is clean, such as donations from unsuspecting charities or individuals or bulk cash, and it will be put to use to fuel the terror operation in some manner. Therefore,

Table. Differences and Similarities between Criminal and Terrorist Money Laundering

	Criminal	Terrorist
Motivation	Greed	Ideology
How money is obtained	Illicit activity	Licit activities such as charities, cash donations, hawala
Purpose	Money is already "dirty," crime has occurred, attempting to make clean	Money is clean, then used for terrorist operations
Cash Amount	Large amounts, many transactions	Small, less frequent transactions
Business	Fronts and shells	Mostly fronts; some shells
Scope	Global; able to fund operations from afar	Global; able to fund operations from afar
Complexity	Hard to tie to operations	Hard to tie to operations

the laundering operations are slightly different in scope and activity, although no less complex and hard to detect. The preceding table of comparison between traditional and terrorist money laundering is based on discussions between the author and agents at the Treasury Department and the FBI.

A good example of small transactions used to fund terror came to light in the government's indictment of Zacarias Moussaoui, the often-alleged "21st hijacker." In this public document, the 9/11 money trail is explained in-depth, along with details of numerous money transfers between al-Qaeda abroad—in the United Arab Emirates (UAE)—and the hijackers in the United States. The amount transferred was usually small, a few thousand dollars at a time, and deposited into a bank account. Oddly, the terrorists meticulously returned small amounts of unused money to the UAE group in the days preceding the attacks. FBI investigators told the author that these transactions were easily detected, and agents then backtracked, thus unraveling the entire 9/11 financing trail.

The use of fronts and shells is another way organized crime and terrorists launder money. Front operations are legitimate businesses whose books are used to wash the money. Often, another operation is going on out the back door such as drug trafficking or prostitution, and the dirty money is pushed back through the legitimate business. It was speculated that bin Laden made extensive use of the "honey house" business in Yemen in this manner to store and move his clean money. An example of how a US firm was possibly used in this manner is the case involving Boston software firm, PTECH, Inc. In late 2002, employees alerted the FBI that a key investor was Yasin al-Qadi, who was on the Treasury Department's list of Specially Designated Global Terrorists. Al-Qadi is a Saudi businessman suspected of diverting millions of dollars to al-Qaeda while at the helm of the charity Blessed Relief Foundation. The case is ongoing, but it appears that his investment in PTECH, Inc. was a way to conceal money to be used for terrorist operations.[37]

A shell is a slightly more complicated business venture; it is a company that does not exist. The simplest form of a shell would be a hotel room (used for its phone) or an empty office space with a fax machine. Criminals set up a toll-free phone number, run an ad in a newspaper or a magazine, and then collect money for a nonexistent service or product; they close the business quickly, staying a step ahead of authorities. In the most complicated form, it could also be an "offshore" venture or investment racket; in the global environment, with communications technology, this is certainly an easy way to raise funds without risk of detection. The Treasury Department investigated reports of offshores that opened and closed immediately prior to 9/11 with speculation in the travel and airline industries; such insider knowledge would mean the offshores were operated by al-Qaeda network. However, Treasury was unable to substantiate these reports. The author spoke with the compliance officer for a major international bank who stated that offshores are an emerging area of concern regarding terrorist moneymaking and laundering.

Worrisome is the scope of laundering in countries bordering the United States. Following 9/11 Canada began to take a hard look at money laundering within its country's borders. The fledgling financial transactions and reports analysis center of Canada (FINTRAC) quickly uncovered $500 million in suspected dirty money stashed away in mutual funds, Canadian banks, and other financial institutions. The Canadian government now estimates that $17 billion worth of criminal proceeds are laundered there each year, and that organized crime costs their taxpayers more than $100 billion annually.[38]

The US government is working to identify and halt terrorist money-laundering efforts. The Treasury Department's 2003 money-laundering strategy focused on alternative ways terrorists may raise or move money, stating, "As the banking system comes under increasing scrutiny, terrorists may turn as well to other mechanisms to transfer funds."[39] According to a Federal Reserve anti-money-laundering examiner, due to the Patriot Act there has been unprecedented cooperation between the domestic and international financial community, law enforcement, and regulators. In the United States this cooperation resulted in a rapid exchange of vital financial information between law enforcement and banks. On an international scale, the efforts of many have caused severe damage to laundering havens and resulted in significant forfeiture and freezing of terrorist assets.[40]

Operation Green Quest was a multiagency task force of law-enforcement agents with financial expertise assembled to investigate how criminals (and terrorists) move their money and where. With the move of Customs under Department of Homeland Security, the team was renamed Operation Cornerstone with the mission to identify and assess the means and methods used by criminals to exploit financial systems to transfer, launder, and otherwise mask the true source of criminal proceeds. Their combined investigations have led to at least 28 indictments and the seizure of about $27.4 million.[41] This renewed focus on money laundering should yield more information regarding similar ongoing terrorist money-laundering activities, and at the very least, serve as a deterrent.

An area of emerging concern is prepaid cards such as phone cards, gift cards, and credit cards that are preloaded and distributed with little or no paper trail. Use of these cards by terrorist and criminal groups would certainly be a convenient, untraceable way to launder money and move value.

Bulk-Cash Smuggling

A less sophisticated way of moving cash is through smuggling. According to the Treasury Department, bulk-cash smuggling refers to moving currency, traveler's checks, or similar instruments across borders by means of a courier rather than through a formal financial system.[42] Although risky in terms of mission failure if detected, bulk- cash smuggling is attractive to terrorists because it is easy to move large quantities of money, there are no paper trails or third parties involved, and the group maintains total control over movement. Also, in the Arab culture, it is not uncommon for individuals to carry a large amount of currency on their person, so bulk cash may not draw attention.

Tightened banking regulations will force terrorists elsewhere to move cash. Juan Zarate, Treasury deputy assistant secretary for terrorist finance and financial crime, stated that the United States has information that al-Qaeda is relying more on couriers because of the crackdown on the traditional banking sector.[43] On 22 December 2003 at least six Arabs, believed to have links to al-Qaeda and carrying what some intelligence reports estimated was $23.5 million, were seized by

41

Syria. It is believed, according to counterterrorism officials, to be the first time in the global war on terrorism that couriers have been apprehended with a large amount of money. While US authorities have also spotted couriers leaving Saudi Arabia and Kuwait, they have not been able to stop them because US officials have no jurisdiction.[44]

Finance ministers and central bank presidents from G-7/8 countries recently discussed ways to deal with the emerging bulk-cash-smuggling problem. One possible option under review is for countries to consider adopting some type of $10,000 reporting requirement similar to the United States. Of course, this law did not stop potential terrorist Zacarias Moussaoui: on 23 February 2001 upon landing in Chicago on a flight originating in London, he simply declared the $35,000 in cash that he had on his person.[45]

Hawalas

Much is written about the use of an informal banking system called "hawala" by terrorists to move money. Attention was focused on the hawala method when it was found that the al-Barakaat informal banking system was used to move funds for al-Qaeda. Informal banking systems are ancient and known by many names reflecting cultural origins. *Hawala*, or *hundi*, are terms commonly used when describing Indian, Pakistani, and Middle Eastern systems. This system is quick (can send money internationally in the same time it takes to place a phone call), easy, and based on trust. The money is not physically moved across any borders; the sender gives the cash to an agent in the United States, who calls an agent at the forward location, who in turn delivers the sum to the recipient. Receipts are not given on either end of the transaction, and no log is kept regarding the identities of the sender and receiver. The amount of money transferred is the only concern; thus, a paper trail is nonexistent. The agents here and abroad work out the monetary issues between themselves to balance their books by transferring goods, paying off other debts, and so forth. The system is unregulated, undocumented, and provides the nontransparency that is desirable to terrorists.

Actions were taken to attempt to regulate this informal, nontraditional transfer system. In the Abu Dhabi declaration on hawala, some Arab states agreed to implement a reporting system. In the UAE, business applications are now required, and Hawaladars are given certificates. The US Patriot Act has a provision requesting that hawalas register, but there is no penalty for failing to register. Of the hundreds located in New York City alone, only 15 hawalas are registered.

As we attempt to inject standards internationally, the cultural significance of this ancient system cannot be overlooked. Islamic banking traditions appeal to Islamic people—they are familiar and trustworthy. For instance, remitters know their money is not being invested in pork, being used for gambling, or in other ways contrary to their faith—concerns that keep them from using the US banking system. Also, many of the areas where relatives of expatriates live are inaccessible by other means, such as Western Union. Western Union charges steep fees, whereas the hawalas are often run concurrent with another business, and the transactions are often done at no cost to the customer. The bottom line is hawalas are not going away, and as we attempt to regulate them, terrorists most likely will find other ways to move their money.

Diamonds: Earning, Moving, and Storing?

According to the GAO, the commodities that terrorists tend to exploit are of high value, easy to conceal, and hold their value over time.[46] The 2003 Money Laundering Strategy further warns "while maintaining our vigilance over traditional means of value transfer, we must also focus on alternative means—trading in commodities such as gold, gems, and precious stones and metals."[47]

The precious stone and metal market is certainly an area susceptible for exploitation. For example, gold's shape can be altered into any form through smelting, an attribute that would be desirable to smugglers. However, diamonds probably serve as the best example of a traded, global commodity that could be exploited by terrorists to earn, move, and store their assets.

43

Douglas Farah, a reporter for the *Washington Post*, broke a story that garnered worldwide attention in December 2002 regarding purported links between al-Qaeda and the diamond market. This connection was widely reported in the press and caused upheaval and concern among those in the diamond industry. Federal law-enforcement agencies have extensively investigated his claims but will neither officially confirm nor deny that his sources exist, that his information is reliable, or that there is an al-Qaeda connection to the diamond industry. However, it is an established fact that al-Qaeda was involved in diamond mining and trading organizations in the early 1990s, and although these operations did not come to fruition, it speaks to their interest and prior knowledge of the industry.[48] There is also widespread, yet unsubstantiated, reporting in the press of a connection between Hezbollah in Lebanon and diamond smugglers in Africa.

Diamonds are especially easy to smuggle because of their low weight. According to the Congressional Research Service, a pound of diamonds in 2002 was worth $225,000 compared to a pound of cash ($45,000) and a pound of gold ($4,800).[49] Diamonds are untraceable, making them more attractive than serial-numbered bills. They are odorless, and thus can be smuggled past working dogs and equipment designed to identify smuggled drugs and money. Diamonds have great value and can easily be used in lieu of cash in business transactions, and diamond mines are located in remote, often lawless areas of Africa. The areas of possible al-Qaeda activity, according to Farah, were the diamond markets of Sierra Leone and Liberia, which, although representing less than 2 percent of the $7 billion global diamond market, have some of the best stones in the world.

Farah's investigation into al-Qaeda financing reported that they started pursuing the diamond market after assets were frozen by the United States following the embassy bombings in 1998.[50] If factual, this supports the theory that as we close traditional funding sources, al-Qaeda and other terrorist entities may move into nontraditional areas to earn, move, and store assets.

Why wouldn't a terrorist group delve into the diamond world? Significant expertise in gemology is an absolute necessity; diamonds exported from Africa are uncut and to the untrained eye, simply appear to be dirty glass. Diamonds are not liquid and easily launderable like money—they must be purchased and sold. Even though paper trails are mostly nonexistent in black-market trade, multiple transactions create witnesses, an undesirable to terrorist organizations. There are significant cultural issues to overcome for the terrorists involved. Those of the Jewish faith dominate the Antwerp diamond market; thus, business activities associated with unloading the diamonds for cash might be a significant hurdle for a traditional Muslim terrorist group.

At the very least, diamonds are certainly traded on the black market and are used by African warlords to fund some of their violent activity, giving advent to the term *blood diamonds*. Forty-five nations (including the United States) met in Switzerland in 2002 to discuss illicit diamond sales and use of profit to pay for weapons in African wars. The State Department appointed an official as special negotiator for issues regarding these "conflict diamonds," and the group developed new regulations for governments of diamond-producing nations. Governments must not only license diamond miners but must also develop "tamper-proof" ways to ship and move rough diamonds across borders. On the buying end, cutting centers (such as those in Antwerp) must ascertain and certify the origin of the rough diamonds. These cutters are the terrorists' last "wicket," as cut and polished diamonds are practically untraceable.[51]

Emerging Area of Concern: Intellectual Property Crime

In July 2003 an Interpol investigator testified at a congressional hearing regarding links between intellectual property crime (IPC) and the financing of terrorism. According to Interpol, intellectual property refers to the legal rights that correspond to intellectual activity in the industrial, scientific, and artistic fields. These legal rights—most commonly in the form of patents, trademarks, and copyrights—protect the moral and economic rights of the creators, in addition to the creativity and dissemination of their work. Based on this understanding, IPC refers to counterfeited and pirated goods that are manufactured and sold for profit without the consent of the patent or trademark holder. IPC is a black-market activity operating parallel to the formal economy and includes manufacturing, transporting, storing, and selling counterfeit or pirated goods. Examples of pirated goods are compact discs (CD), digital video or versatile discs (DVD), cigarettes, clothes, shoes, designer purses, and computer software.

IPC is occurring throughout the world and generates unbelievable amount of profits for perpetrators. Counterfeit-goods trade is estimated at $450 billion, representing 5 to 7 percent of the of global trade value. The FBI estimates US business losses to counterfeiting alone at $200 to $250 billion annually. IPC is a lucrative criminal activity with low initial investment and high financial returns, possibly even higher than drug trafficking. For example, a Nintendo game costs $0.20 to duplicate and is resold for $40, thus recognizing enormous profit. IPC is also a low-risk activity; law-enforcement agencies do not have or choose to expend resources to pursue it, and if caught, the prison sentence for an offender is light. The link between organized crime groups and counterfeit goods is well established, but Interpol's testimony sounds the alarm that IPC is a global criminal activity on the rise and is becoming a lucrative method of funding for a number of terrorist groups.

Several regions are particularly susceptible to IPC. Large portions of consumer goods for sale in Kosovo are counterfeit. The sales openly occur, and there is limited enforcement of existing laws. In Kosovo there is a long-standing relationship between criminal organizations and ethnic-Albanian extremist groups. It is suspected that funds generated from IPC benefit both criminal organizations and these extremist groups. In 2000 a joint operation between Russian law-enforcement agencies and private industry resulted in the breakup of a CD manufacturing plant run by an organized crime group, which was remitting funds to Chechen rebels. Several North African groups operating in Europe receive profits from IPC through charitable giving, laundered through *zakat* via mosques, imams, or nonprofit organizations sympathetic to radical fundamentalist causes. In this example, terrorists do not engage in the IPC; they just reap the profits, making this an even less risky venture.

International terrorist groups are turning to IPC to fund their operations. In late 2000 a container of counterfeit perfume, creams, cologne, and shampoos was shipped by a member of al-Qaeda from Dubai and intercepted by Danish customs in Copenhagen. Further investigation showed that al-Qaeda sought to profit from the sale of these counterfeit items. Hezbollah funding comes from as far away as South America. In February 2000 an individual was arrested in the tri-border region of South America selling pirated music and game CDs and using profits to fund a Hezbollah-related organization in Lebanon. In a true example of exploitation of the global market, the goods were produced in Europe and sent to a free-trade zone in South America by Hezbollah sympathizers, further identified as Lebanese criminals. Smuggling the goods to a third country in South America avoided import duties and taxes, and sales were provided through a network of Middle East militants and sympathizers.[52]

Why might IPC become a more important source of illicit financing for terrorist groups? According to Interpol, lacking sufficient resources or technical investigative knowledge, law enforcement does not treat IPC as a high priority crime. If the crime is acknowledged, the result is often seizure of goods or halting of production, with no further investigation of the money trail. The money trail is complex with cash-based transactions, which make this a desirable endeavor to terrorist groups. Trafficking in counterfeit goods is a relatively easy criminal activity. A terrorist could profit solely from the sale of counterfeit or pirated goods and does not need to be involved in the production or fabrication. Thus, entry costs are relatively low, and the illicit profit margins are high. It follows that the profiteer risk ratio is attractive not only to criminals but also to loosely networked terrorist groups who do not have the capacity to generate funds through sophisticated criminal activity. Wide ranges of products are vulnerable to IPC, and demand is widespread due to public perception that purchasing these goods is not criminal. Think of the numerous vendor stands found in big cities, hawking knock-off designer purses, scarves, and sunglasses that bear the same logos and can only be identified as fakes by the trained eye. This low-risk/high-return activity and others like it bear watching as we close down other sources of terrorist funding.

Notes

1. CSIS, "Transnational Threats Update."
2. Cilluffo, "The Threat Posed from the Convergence of Organized Crime, Drug Trafficking, and Terrorism."
3. Ibid.
4. Clarke, "The Financing of Terror Organizations."
5. Cowell, "Terrorism's Cost in a Global Economy."
6. Noble, "The Links between Intellectual Property Crime and Terrorist Financing."
7. Brisard, *Terrorism Financing.*
8. GAO, "Federal Agencies Face Continuing Challenges in Addressing Terrorist Financing and Money Laundering."
9. Cowell, "45 Nations Set to Back Rules on Illicit Diamond Trading."
10. Vistica, "Frozen Assets Going to Legal Bills."
11. "Treasury Revokes Tax-Exempt Status of 3 Muslim Charities."
12. *United States of America vs Enaam M. Arnaout.*
13. GAO, "Terrorist Financing."
14. *Global Relief Foundation, Inc. v. Paul H. O'Neill, Colin L. Powell, John Ashcroft, R. Richard Newcomb, and Robert S. Mueller III.*
15. Al-Haramain Foundation, "Al-Haramain Was Shut Down by the Saudi Government Because of a Charge of Funding Islamic Terrorism."
16. Waller, "D.C. Islamist Agent Carried Libyan Cash."
17. Dilanian, "U.N. Report Finds Two Terror Financiers Living, Doing Business Freely."
18. Vistica, "Frozen Assets Going to Legal Bills."
19. CSIS, "Canadian Agency Finds Dirty Money."
20. Bush, "Statement of the President."
21. Cilluffo, "The Threat Posed from the Convergence of Organized Crime, Drug Trafficking, and Terrorism."
22. Ibid.
23. Drug Enforcement Administration, "Drugs and Terror."
24. Arab Press, "The Role of Fatwas in Incitement to Terrorism."
25. Cilluffo, "The Threat Posed from the Convergence of Organized Crime, Drug Trafficking, and Terrorism."
26. Ibid.
27. Scarborough, "Drug Money Sustains al-Qaeda."

28. Cilluffo, "The Threat Posed from the Convergence of Organized Crime, Drug Trafficking, and Terrorism."

29. Denny, *Terrorism, Drug Trafficking Inextricably Linked, US Experts Say.*

30. "Drug Ring Linked to Terror."

31. CSIS, "Canadian Agency Finds Dirty Money."

32. O'Harrow, "Identity Crisis."

33. Ibid.

34. "Fraud, ID Theft Finance Terror."

35. Ibid.

36. Wikipedia, *The Free Encyclopedia.*

37. Seper, "US Agents Raid Software Firm, Seeking al-Qaeda Money Link."

38. CSIS, "Canadian Agency Finds Dirty Money."

39. Aversa, "U.S. to Sharpen Focus on Terror Funding."

40. "Federal Reserve Examiner Spreads Knowledge to Global Audience."

41. Anderson, "Terror Investigators Raid Mass. Company."

42. GAO, "Federal Agencies Face Continuing Challenges in Addressing Terrorist Financing and Money Laundering."

43. Aversa, "Nations to Discuss Ways to Cut Off Terrorists' Financing."

44. Farah, "Syria Seizes Six Arab Couriers, $23 Million."

45. *United States of America v. Zacarias Moussaoui.*

46. GAO, "Federal Agencies Face Continuing Challenges in Addressing Terrorist Financing and Money Laundering."

47. Departments of Treasury and Justice, "2003 National Money Laundering Strategy."

48. GAO, "Terrorist Financing: US Agencies Should Systematically Assess Terrorists' Use of Alternative Financing Mechanisms."

49. Ibid.

50. Farah, "Report Says Africans Harbored al-Qaeda: Terror Assets Hidden in Gem-Buying Spree."

51. Cowell, "45 Nations Set to Back Rules on Illicit Diamond Trading."

52. Noble, "The Links between Intellectual Property Crime and Terrorist Financing."

Chapter 4

Terrorist Groups: Corporate Trends

Surely, it is no coincidence that the threat to the stability and peace of the world has coincided with the globalization of technology, transportation, commerce, and communication. The same benefits enjoyed by peace-loving people across the world are available to terrorists as well.

—Secretary Tom Ridge
Department of Homeland Security
9 March 2004

As the world changes, so will the ways terrorist groups organize, equip, plan, train, and execute their agendas. According to a November 2003 GAO study, US intelligence agencies have identified trends related to international terrorism.[1] By first stating these trends from the report, then factoring in all of the elements previously discussed in this study, it is possible to speculate as to the corporate trend in international terrorist groups.

Decline in State-Sponsored Terrorism

Terrorists are less dependent on sponsorship by sovereign states. State sponsors provide political, financial, and logistical support and a safe haven for terrorists. State sponsors have provided intelligence, planning, and support for terrorist acts and may have had prior knowledge of such attacks. However, threats of sanctions and retaliation have reduced the willingness of most states to sponsor terrorism. By the late 1990s, according to the director of the Central Intelligence Agency, a completely new phenomenon had emerged—terrorists sponsoring a state.

The same factors that gave rise to transnational crime also fuel the terrorist agenda: technology and globalization mean that terrorists do not need support from a traditional nation-state, ideologically or logistically. In fighting the global war on terror, we engage at the nation-state level by asking them not to support terrorist activities on their soil; however, their course of action when attempting to comply varies, as does their success. For example, rather than treat the problem as a national crisis, previous state sponsor Colombia annexed FARC, which gave them their own territory and virtual autonomy. Therefore, any restraints previously imposed on FARC by Colombia have now disappeared, thus strengthening and allowing the group to operate corporately and expand transnationally. Afghanistan is not sponsoring terror but seems unable to deal with its ever-increasing poppy crop, which continues to fuel terrorist groups inside and outside of its borders. As the United States tries to thwart state-sponsored terror, traditional state-based engagement alone may not deter or unravel terrorist operations, and diplomatic efforts may be fruitless unless applied in a nontraditional or asymmetric manner.

Engaging terrorist groups instead of nation-states is a horrifying prospect to most diplomats, but it may be an inevitable reality. One expert stated that al-Qaeda is as much an ideology as a structure.[2] As radical ideologies take hold and spread internationally with parent groups leveraging communications technology to reach nearly everyone on the globe who has the Internet, a television, or a radio, the seed will be planted without nation-state support and possibly even without their knowledge. The nation-state is completely irrelevant to these groups; more important are the followers who adhere to the ideology. Communism was neatly constrained by borders, and thus engagement with nation-states was successful. To fight this battle—in the global realm—will not be easy.

Move to Loosely Affiliated Groups: Franchising

As dependency on state-sponsored terrorism decreases, terrorist groups operating alone in loosely affiliated groups have increased. The resulting transnational and decentralized structure facilitates terrorists avoiding detection. Islamic terrorist groups appear loosely organized, recruit their membership from many different countries, and obtain support from an informal international network of like-minded extremists.

The decentralization and fracturing of al-Qaeda as a result of operations in Afghanistan is a good example of how an established, successful group can remain deadly despite state-based operations to rid them. Decimation implies taking of the top 10 percent; in a typical military campaign, it is believed that decimation leads to success. However, decimating al-Qaeda (which we have done, with the exception of Osama bin Laden) has not prevented the group from operating successfully. An ideology cannot be decimated.

The franchising of terror requires greater study. The splinter factions of al-Qaeda have leaders who were most likely trained in al-Qaeda camps, and they have learned well from their master. One senior US official reportedly said al-Qaeda's children were "growing up and moving out into the world, loyal to their parents but no longer reliant on them."[3] Communication between these groups has also increased, and US and European intelligence analysts said they also recognize similarities in the groups' communication techniques and tactics regarding the use of explosives. Recent attacks for which al-Qaeda groups took responsibility or have been suspected of executing have a modus operandi that continues to be synchronized, stealthy, deadly, and low-budget. These groups are all that remain of al-Qaeda and bear the burden of continuing the war against the infidels.

The regional aspect of these loosely affiliated groups is an important point when discussing financial structure. Rather than facing a few defined, recognized targets and long money trails, we now must face small, dispersed groups. Taking out one avenue of financing will not have the same crippling effect it had before. One senior US official stated, "Now, groups in Indonesia raise money there. Groups in Malaysia raise money there. There are many more targets and much harder to find."[4] These groups rely on petty crime, drug trafficking, and extortion to pay the bills. Complicating the problem are the softer targets in attacks that require less sophistication and money to execute.

The shift to human capital is an important point, according to officials. "Many of these cells don't appear to be very well-funded, but what is more important than money is human capital. And human capital doesn't seem to be in short supply."[5] This human capital can be gained from a close association with organized crime.

Michael Pillsbury, a Pentagon terrorism consultant, argues that the evolution of the terrorist groups is analogous to a process of corporate merger and acquisition, where regionally focused terrorist groups with their own agendas join with al-Qaeda to learn their operational techniques or benefit from their contacts, but are not subordinate to al-Qaeda. For example, he said, Jemaah Islamiyah seeks to create a pan-Islamic state in Asia, an agenda that has little to do with driving US forces out of Saudi Arabia or other goals of bin Laden's. "They like to get advice and equipment from al-Qaeda but still have their own political agenda."[6] Perhaps a comparison can be drawn to Cuba's relationship with the former Union of Soviet Socialist Republics. The ideology has taken hold, so the fall of the "business headquarters" of al-Qaeda will not lead to all of its franchises closing shop.

Shifting Tactics

Tactics among international terrorists have shifted from aircraft hijackings and hostage taking to indiscriminate terrorist attacks that yield maximum destruction, casualties, and impact. Although the vast majority of terrorist attacks worldwide continue to be carried out with conventional weapons, such as firearms and bombs, there is concern among US intelligence community officials about terrorists using unconventional weapons, such as weapons of mass destruction to include chemical, biological, radiological, or nuclear weapons.

International terrorist groups are moving to loosely affiliated groups or franchises. Shifting tactics may be a related phenomenon. Smaller cells may take less time to plan or have less patience than that exhibited in previous attacks; but if they sense detection, it may even lead to a dangerous desperation to go operational quickly.

A shift from long-range to short-range planning may be worrisome; *time* is the major resource needed by officials who track terrorists as they unravel their complex funding and logistical schemes and connect the dots. Alternatively, it could lead to carelessness and failure to cover tracks and could enable quicker detection. Regardless, the trend is that tactics have shifted, and it is the difficult job of law enforcement and intelligence agencies to adjust their efforts accordingly.

Alliance with Transnational Crime

There has been a coalescence of terrorism with other transnational crimes, which provides terrorists with various ways to finance their operations. These include illegal immigration, contraband smuggling, visa fraud, piracy, illegal trafficking in human beings, diamond smuggling, tobacco diversion, and associated tax fraud.

All of the previous trends point to this one conclusion: decline in state sponsorship, the franchising of terrorist groups, and shifting tactics will lead terrorists to increased partnering with organized crime. Critics argue that terrorists' ideology prevents or prohibits them from such an alliance, to which one could point out the numerous narco-terror connections that have been major successes. Although all criminals are not terrorists, all terrorists are criminals; they coexist and operate in the same domain with similar methods. However, the likelihood of their increased liaison is greatly debated within our government agencies.

Would Terrorists and Organized Crime Partner?

Even though terrorist groups already have some ties with organized crime, will they increasingly seek criminals' assistance and form greater alliances? This question was posed in several off-the-record interviews with federal agents involved in organized crime and/or tracking terrorist financing. Their answers provide excellent context for the continued study of trends and emerging funding sources for terrorists.

Why Terrorists and Organized Crime Partner:

- Money talks. Criminals do not care what you are moving or the reason—if you can pay, they will do the job for you.

- Terrorists have already shown that conflicting ideologies will not prevent them from such an alliance. The example of the Mafia illustrates this point; 10 years ago, Mafia leaders publicly stated that they would never get into the drug business. They also said they would never do business with African Americans. Yet the two activities are prevalent in today's IOC syndicates. No method of earning, moving, or storing assets is off the table because of ideology.

- Manpower—the two need it, and both have it.

- Established networks are tough to crack, especially in the narcotics realm. This connection makes continued alliance in drug trafficking likely.

- Organized crime has established infrastructure, which provides low overhead that conserves money for the terrorist attack.

- The seductiveness of the amount of resources and unlimited supply (particularly in drugs and humans) is hard to resist. With ideology distorted, terrorists themselves may become users of these commodities. The Afghan president recently expressed his concern about the emerging problem of a rise of heroin and opium use in the country.[7] An Afghani source with extensive experience with in-country eradication efforts told the author that cultivators, traffickers, and profit takers are now users and addicts—an alarming trend that will negatively impact efforts to obliterate the poppy crop in Afghanistan.

- Because we are effectively closing the door on methods like charities and *hawala*, terrorists may soon have no alternative and must turn to organized crime.

Why Terrorists and Organized Crime Do Not Partner:

- Too many people involved in transactions; terrorists prefer anonymity, and the fewer people involved, the less chance of mission failure.

- Organized crime does not want to knowingly "get in bed" with terrorists for business reasons. It brings unwanted attention. Why become involved with groups that the US government is using extensive resources to pursue and possibly destroy your successful business?

- Some organized crime members are "good Americans" and were deeply affected by 9/11, particularly in New York City. They do not want to be responsible or culpable for further terrorist attacks.

- Organized crime does not need the terrorist business. The criminals are doing quite well alone.

- Organized crime does not want to share business.

- These criminals are not natural allies since their motivations differ.

- Organized crime is in the profit-taking and profit-making business; after paying people and debts, profits are recycled into the operation, and the criminal activity continues. For terrorists, especially local cells, the crime is a means to an end. The criminals are only in business until the attack is successfully executed, then they are out.

As the debate continues, modern transnational criminals and terrorists are seeking new ways to obtain resources to fuel their expensive operations. Their continued and expanded liaison appears inevitable.

Notes

1. GAO, "Terrorist Financing: US Agencies Should Systematically Assess Terrorists' Use of Alternative Financing Mechanisms."
2. Farah, "Terrorism Inc.: Al-Qaeda Franchises Brand of Violence to Groups across World."
3. Ibid.
4. Ibid.
5. Ibid.
6. Ibid.
7. Berniker, "Afghanistan Stands on Brink of Becoming 'Narco-State.'"

Chapter 5

Conclusion: The Battle at the Crossroads

At 12:01 A.M. this morning, a major thrust of our war on terrorism began with the stroke of a pen. Today, we have launched a strike on the financial foundation of the global terror network. Money is the lifeblood of terrorist operations. Today, we're asking the world to stop payment.

—Pres. George W. Bush
Introducing Executive Order 13224
24 September 2001

There are forces we cannot change such as globalization, technological progress, shifting demographics, geopolitical issues, and religious ideology—we can only adapt and learn to coexist. Consequently, whether combating transnational crime or terrorism, *containment* and *deterrence* strategies must be woven into the battle plan. Criminals and terrorists operate in an underworld that is opaque and often impenetrable; learning to live with unresolved ambiguity in the face of such an enemy is requisite. These concepts may be unpopular with policy makers and implementers, but reality deems them a necessity.

Much research has been conducted on transnational crime and terrorist financing; however, the criminal-terrorist nexus requires more analysis. Very few individuals have expertise regarding the nexus, and little subject matter is available to researchers. It is rarely acknowledged as an emerging issue that demands a fresh look and unique solutions.

Regarding the nexus, Cilluffo accurately points out that "only an integrated strategy that synchronizes the various organizational efforts under a unifying concept can address these problems. Such a strategy would integrate intelligence collection, linked to the full range of consumers in support of a variety of operational actions—not just eradication but also diplomatic efforts, law-enforcement activities, covert action, and military action."[1]

The US military, which operates in nearly every global region, can be a force multiplier in the fight against transnational organized crime and terrorist funding. Military personnel do not receive adequate training on terrorism and terrorist groups. Training is targeted to those deploying, those attending professional military education courses, and limited other audiences. This study recommends distribution of basic information to all military members (see the appendix) and annual refresher training that provides updates as groups alter form and strategies. Forces on the ground who already interact with the local populace can be taught to recognize laundering, trafficking, and smuggling tactics and must be educated on emerging methods, as well as the aforementioned "vacuum" in institutions formed following a government revolution and associated vulnerabilities. Commanders must have greater knowledge of these activities in their area of operation, with robust tie-in to federal agencies simultaneously conducting in-theater operations.

Integration of organized crime and terrorism fighters requires information and resource sharing on a scale previously unseen. Government agencies must continue to put cultural differences aside and capitalize on what each brings to the fight. It appears that at the tactical level, post–9/11 integration has been effective, particularly the FBI's Joint Terrorism Task Force that integrates federal agencies such as the DEA and the Bureau of Alcohol, Tobacco, Firearms and Explosives at the local level. However, at the strategic level, information sharing is less frequent. Several senior-level, cross-agency working groups formed after the terrorist attacks are now defunct or only meet on an as-needed basis. As scarce resources are expended on battling international terrorism, government agencies must continue to address parallel, seemingly unrelated activities with domestic terror groups. The environment is ripe for an alliance between the two.

Federal agents must continue to have robust support for their law-enforcement activities. The Patriot Act granted expanded authority, delegated certain responsibilities, and streamlined bureaucratic procedures. Fighting modern organized crime and terrorism in the global environment demands this type of investigative and operational support, and revoking or drastically altering the Patriot Act is a step in the wrong direction. Expanded training for agents in nontraditional, proactive investigative procedures to identify and prevent the crime or terrorist act before it occurs is also a necessity.

In a war where a bank teller may be the first line of defense in terror financing, this battle requires new partnering between the private sector, the business world, and the US government. Fostering new interest and expertise in "financial forensics" is a must, and if practitioners also have an understanding of organized crime and terrorist funding, the practitioners will be a powerful weapon in the fight against the growing nexus.

This research proposes scholarly study regarding the life cycle of modern terrorist groups. The advent of modern terrorism is widely acknowledged to have begun in 1968 with a rash of airline hijackings and assassinations. A chronological, comparative analysis of terrorist group activity since 1968 may yield clues as to when and why, despite religious ideology, terrorists partner with organized crime. By removing the mystery, philosophizing, and uncertainty from the study of terrorist groups and instead, approaching the issue scientifically, related law-enforcement efforts may become predictive instead of reactive in nature.

Mass media can be used as a vehicle to alert the public of emerging terrorist-funding methods, such as IPC. Associating the purchasing of counterfeit goods to the war on terror, similar to the DEA's antidrug campaign after 9/11, may proactively deny its viability as a financing source.

Asymmetric engagement must be employed as a tool in the fight against growing transnational crime and terrorism. The traditional nation-state approach will not be enough as groups assume the same characteristics as multinational corporations—transcending borders, leveraging technology, and changing tactics effortlessly. Marginalizing their impact on the world and delegitimizing their activities by negating the desired effects on the global audience are two ways to contain and deter. Another option is to directly engage the "silent majority" of Muslims, asking for their intervention and collaboration of solutions, instead of imposing our will and culture similar to unsuccessful efforts to regulate *hawalas*. Addressing the concerns of the global Muslim community, such as poverty, displacement, and ideological disillusionment may diminish its value as a fertile recruiting ground for terror. Use of the "soft" instruments of power may deem more valuable than the use of military force. A renewed appreciation of cultural differences and focus on similarities are key in any negotiation and can be done without either side validating the other's as superior. A true dialogue concerning religious ideologies and how to coexist in modern society is a must. Greater use of respected institutions such as the UN may open the door to a new solution set that the policy makers may presently overlook.

Although no effort can prevent a lone terrorist from strapping on explosives and entering a busy marketplace, we must remember that in the case of al-Qaeda, the mission is not to simply disrupt our way of life or economy, it is to ultimately destroy the Great Satan and its allies—an apocalyptic agenda that requires major funding to execute. Therefore, as with all national security endeavors, the government must be willing to execute a robust and aggressive strategy with the worse-case scenario omnipresent. Our nation deserves and expects no less.

Notes

1. Cilluffo, "The Threat Posed from the Convergence of Organized Crime, Drug Trafficking, and Terrorism."

Appendix

Multinational Corporation Terrorist Groups: A Primer

Information derived from the Council on Foreign Relations Terrorism Web site: http://www.cfrterrorism.org/groups.

Abu Sayyaf Group. Abu Sayyaf (the phrase means "bearer of the sword" in Arabic) is a militant organization based in the southern Philippines seeking a separate Islamic state for the country's Muslim minority. The White House says Abu Sayyaf is a terrorist organization with ties to Osama bin Laden's al-Qaeda network.

Abu Sayyaf operates mostly in the southern Philippines, where most of the country's Muslims live and where the group has its base. But Abu Sayyaf has acted in other parts of the Philippines, and in 2000, its members crossed the Sulu Sea to Malaysia for a kidnapping.

Abu Sayyaf formed during a split from the Moro National Liberation Front, one of the two major Muslim separatist movements in the southern Philippines, which were then trying to come to terms with the central government in Manila. The group's first major attack came in 1991, when an Abu Sayyaf grenade killed two American evangelists. Its first leader was Abdurajak Janjalani, a Philippine Muslim who fought in the international Islamist brigade in Afghanistan during the Soviet occupation. In 1998 Aburajak Janjalani died in a confrontation with the Philippine police. His brother Khadafi Janjalani then became the nominal leader of Abu Sayyaf, but the group has since split into several factions.

Muhammad Jamal Khalifa, the Saudi who helped fund Abu Sayyaf, is also Osama bin Laden's brother-in-law. In the late 1980s, Khalifa reportedly urged Abu Sayyaf founder Janjalani to fight in Afghanistan and funneled money from Persian Gulf donors to Abu Sayyaf through Islamic charities. Abu Sayyaf claimed responsibility for a 1994 bomb that was planted under a passenger seat on a Philippine airlines jet; this bombing, which killed a Japanese businessman, was a test run for a 1995 plot to simultaneously blow up 11 US passenger jetliners over the Pacific Ocean. This scheme, which was foiled before it could be carried out, has been traced to Ramzi Yousef, the mastermind of the 1993 bombing of the World Trade Center, who reportedly had ties with Khalifa.

Abu Sayyaf's crimes include bombings, assassinations, kidnappings, and extortion. In May 2001 Abu Sayyaf kidnapped 20 people, including three Americans, at a Philippine resort and demanded ransom payments. Abu Sayyaf beheaded one of the American captives and held the other two Americans—a Christian missionary couple—hostage on Basilan Island in the southern Philippines. In June 2002 US-trained Philippine commandos tried to rescue the couple and a Filipino nurse being held with them. Two of the hostages were killed in the shootout, and one, the American missionary Gracia Burnham, was freed. In August 2002 Abu Sayyaf kidnapped six Filipino Jehovah's Witnesses and beheaded two of them. Abu Sayyaf targets Americans: "We have been trying hard to get an American because they may think we are afraid of them," a spokesman for Abu Sayyaf said. "We want to fight the American people." Abu Sayyaf has also captured local business people and Philippine schoolchildren, but Western hostages make for larger ransom payments.

The governments of the United States and the Philippines suspect Abu Sayyaf is part of al-Qaeda, and the United States says Abu Sayyaf helps coordinate al-Qaeda activity in Southeast Asia. But longtime observers of the Philippines say that Abu Sayyaf's goals may not be identical with those of bin Laden.

In the aftermath of the 9/11 attacks, the United States sent about 650 troops to advise the Philippine soldiers pursuing Abu Sayyaf and train them on new equipment and intelligence techniques; that mission ended in July 2002. The George W. Bush administration proposed sending US combat troops to the Philippines in March 2003 but downgraded their assignment to training and intelligence work in the face of widespread public opposition. The State Department formally designated Abu Sayyaf a terrorist organization in 1997, which allowed the US government to freeze any assets the group had in the United States.

Abu Haf al-Masri Brigades. An Abu Sayyaf Group offshoot named after Mohammed Atef, a terrorist who was wanted for the 1998 embassy bombings in Africa and killed by the CIA on 15 November 2001 by a Hellfire missile. The group claimed responsibility for synagogue bombings in Islamabad on 15 November 2003, killing 30. The same group asserted responsibility for the car bombing at the UN headquarters in Baghdad 19 August 2003 in which 23 people died and said it caused the 14 August 2003 power blackout across the northeastern United States and Canada. They took credit for the 11 March 2004 bombings in Spain that killed more than 200 and injured more than 2,000. They are quick to take credit for bombings and have listed demands.

Al-Qaeda. This group is an international terrorist network led by Osama bin Laden. It seeks to rid Muslim countries of what it sees as the profane influence of the West and replace their governments with fundamentalist Islamic regimes. After al-Qaeda's 9/11 attacks on America, the United States launched a war in Afghanistan to destroy al-Qaeda's bases there and to overthrow the Taliban, the country's Muslim fundamentalist rulers who harbored bin Laden and his followers. The term *al-Qaeda* is Arabic for the term *the base*.

Al-Qaeda grew out of the Services Office, a clearinghouse for the international Muslim brigade opposed to the 1979 Soviet invasion of Afghanistan. In the 1980s the Services Office—run by bin Laden and the Palestinian religious scholar Abdullah Azzam—recruited, trained, and financed thousands of foreign *mujahedeen*, or holy warriors, from more than 50 countries. Bin Laden wanted these fighters to continue the "holy war" beyond Afghanistan. He formed al-Qaeda around 1988.

According to a 1998 federal indictment, al-Qaeda is administered by a council that discusses and approves major undertakings, including terrorist operations. At the top is bin Laden. Ayman al-Zawahiri, the head of Egyptian Islamic Jihad, is thought to be bin Laden's top lieutenant and al-Qaeda's ideological adviser. At least one senior al-Qaeda commander, Muhammad Atef, died in the US air strikes in Afghanistan, and another top lieutenant, Abu Zubaydah, was captured in Pakistan in March 2002. In March 2003 the alleged mastermind of the 9/11 attacks, Khalid Shaikh Muhammad, and al-Qaeda's treasurer, Mustafa Ahmed al-Hawsawi, were also captured in Pakistan.

From 1991 to 1996, al-Qaeda worked out of Sudan. From 1996 until the collapse of the Taliban in 2001, al-Qaeda operated out of Afghanistan and maintained its training camps there. US intelligence officials now think al-Qaeda's senior leadership is trying to regroup in lawless tribal regions just inside Pakistan, near the Afghan border, or inside Pakistani cities. Al-Qaeda has autonomous underground cells in 100 countries, including the United States, officials say. Law enforcement has broken up al-Qaeda cells in the United Kingdom, the United States, Italy, France, Spain, Germany, Albania, Uganda, and elsewhere.

Al-Qaeda is connected to the following terrorist groups: Egyptian Islamic Jihad, Jamaat Islamiyya (Egypt), the Libyan Islamic Fighting Group, Islamic Army of Aden (Yemen), Lashkar-e-Taiba and Jaish-e-Muhammad (Kashmir), Islamic Movement of Uzbekistan, Salafist Group for Call and Combat and the Armed Islamic Group (Algeria), and Abu Sayyaf Group (Malaysia, Philippines).

These groups share al-Qaeda's Sunni Muslim fundamentalist views. Some terror experts theorize that al-Qaeda, after the loss of its Afghanistan base, may be increasingly reliant on sympathetic affiliates to carry out its agenda. Intelligence officials and terrorism experts also say that al-Qaeda has stepped-up its cooperation on logistics and training with Hezbollah, a radical, Iran-backed Lebanese militia drawn from the minority Shiite strain of Islam.

Major attacks: The group has targeted American and other Western interests as well as Jewish targets and Muslim governments it saw as corrupt or impious—above all, the Saudi monarchy. Major al-Qaeda-linked attacks include:

- The May 2003 car bomb attacks on three residential compounds in Riyadh, Saudi Arabia

- The November 2002 car bomb attack and a failed attempt to shoot down an Israeli jetliner with shoulder-fired missiles, both in Mombasa, Kenya

- The October 2002 attack on a French tanker off the coast of Yemen. Several spring 2002 bombings in Pakistan

- The April 2002 explosion of a fuel tanker outside a synagogue in Tunisia

- The 11 September 2001, hijacking attacks on the World Trade Center and the Pentagon

- The October 2000 USS *Cole* bombing and the August 1998 bombings of the US embassies in Nairobi, Kenya, and Dar es Salaam, Tanzania

Al-Qaeda is suspected of carrying out or directing sympathetic groups to carry out the March 2004 train bombings in Spain; May 2003 suicide attacks on Western interests in Casablanca, Morocco; the October 2002 nightclub bombing in Bali, Indonesia; and the 1993 World Trade Center bombing. Plots linked to al-Qaeda that were disrupted or prevented include: a 2001 attempt by Richard Reid to explode a shoe bomb on a transatlantic flight; a 1999 plot to set off a bomb at Los Angeles International Airport; a 1995 plan to blow up 12 transpacific flights of US commercial airliners; a 1995 plan to kill President William J. "Bill" Clinton on a visit to the Philippines; and a 1994 plot to kill Pope John Paul II during a visit to Manila.

HAMAS: In Arabic the word *HAMAS* means zeal. But it is also an Arabic acronym for Harakat al-Muqawama al-Islamiya or Islamic Resistance Movement. HAMAS is the Palestinians' major Muslim fundamentalist movement. With an extensive social-service network and a terrorist wing that plots suicide bombings in Israel, it is the main opposition to Yasir Arafat's Palestinian Authority, a determined foe of Israeli-Palestinian peace and a major player in the current Middle East crisis.

HAMAS combines the ideas of Palestinian nationalism and religious fundamentalism. Its founding charter pledges the group to carry out armed struggles, try to destroy Israel, and replace Arafat's government with an Islamist state on the West Bank and Gaza, and raise "the banner of Allah over every inch of Palestine." HAMAS grew out of the Muslim Brotherhood, a religious and political organization founded in Egypt and with branches throughout the Arab world. When a Palestinian uprising against Israeli rule over the West Bank and Gaza broke out in late 1987, HAMAS activists in the Gaza Strip quickly began handing out leaflets and encouraging the newborn intifada.

The first HAMAS suicide bombing took place in April 1993, a few months before the Oslo accords—the main Israeli-Palestinian peace pact—were sealed with the famous September 1993 handshake between Arafat and the then-Israeli prime minister Yitzhak Rabin on the White House lawn. Since 1994 HAMAS and Islamic Jihad have dispatched more than 80 suicide bombers. The terrorists have blown up buses in major Israeli cities, as well as shopping malls, cafes, and other civilian targets. The bombings have killed 377 Israeli civilians and wounded thousands, according to the Israeli government. HAMAS's bombers tend to target civilians within Israel proper, rather than Israeli soldiers or settlers in the West Bank and Gaza. HAMAS has reportedly begun using military-grade explosives in suicide bombings, which makes them more lethal.

HAMAS operates out of the Gaza Strip and the West Bank, two of the world's most hotly disputed pieces of land. Most of the population of these areas is governed by the Palestinian Authority, an autonomous governmental body run by Arafat; most of the land, however, is either partially or completely controlled by Israel, which took Gaza and the West Bank during the Six-Day War in 1967. Since 1993, when Israel and the PLO signed a peace treaty, major Palestinian cities in the West Bank and Gaza have been turned over to the Arafat-run Palestinian Authority.

Its political leadership was headed by Sheik Ahmed Yassin, the group's founder; Yassin, who was released from an Israeli jail in 1997 by then-prime minister Benjamin Netanyahu, was killed in an Israeli air strike on 22 March 2004.

Much of HAMAS's funding comes from Palestinian expatriates, as well as from private donors in Saudi Arabia and other oil-rich Persian Gulf states. Iran also provides significant support, which some diplomats say could amount to between $20 and $30 million per year. Moreover, some Muslim charities in the United States, Canada, and Western Europe funnel money into HAMAS-backed social service groups. In December 2001 the Bush administration seized the assets of the Holy Land Foundation, the largest Muslim charity in the United States, for allegedly funding HAMAS.

Hezbollah: Hezbollah is a Lebanese group of Shiite militants that has evolved into a major force in Lebanon's society and politics. It opposes the West, seeks to create a Muslim fundamentalist state modeled on Iran, and is a bitter foe of Israel. The group's name means "party of God."

Hezbollah and its affiliates have planned or been linked to a lengthy series of terrorist attacks against America, Israel, and other Western targets. These attacks include:

- A series of kidnappings of Westerners, including several Americans, in the 1980s;

- The suicide truck bombings that killed more than 200 US Marines at their barracks in Beirut, Lebanon, in 1983;

- The 1985 hijacking of TWA flight 847, which featured the famous footage of the plane's pilot leaning out of the cockpit with a gun to his head;

- Two major 1990s attacks on Jewish targets in Argentina—the 1992 bombing of the Israeli embassy (killing 29) and the 1994 bombing of a Jewish community center (killing 95).

Hezbollah is sponsored by Iran and Syria. The group receives "substantial amounts of financial, training, weapons, explosives, political, diplomatic, and organizational aid from Iran and Syria," the State Department reports. Hezbollah was founded as a "cats paw" for Iran, Middle East experts say. While Iran gave Hezbollah more funding and support in the 1980s than in the 1990s, it still often gives Hezbollah its orders and its ideological inspiration. And because Lebanon has been under Syrian control since 1990, Hezbollah could not operate in Lebanon without Syria's approval, Middle East experts say. Experts say Hezbollah is also an important player in Lebanon's politics, a key vehicle of Lebanese Shiite empowerment, and a major provider of social services to thousands of Lebanese Shiites.

Hezbollah's base is in Lebanon's Shiite-dominated areas, including parts of Beirut, southern Lebanon, and the Bekaa Valley. US intelligence reports say that Hezbollah cells operate in regions including Europe, Africa, South America, and North America. Despite Israel's 2000 withdrawal from Lebanon, Hezbollah continues to shell Israeli forces at a disputed border area called Shebaa Farms.

Is Hezbollah a "terrorist group of global reach"? In his 20 September 2001 speech to Congress, President Bush pledged that the US-led war on terror "will not end until every terrorist group of global reach has been found, stopped, and defeated." Hezbollah's cells outside the Middle East, its reported involvement in the January 2002 attempt to smuggle a boatload of arms to the Palestinian Authority, and its role in the 1992 and 1994 attacks in Argentina imply that it might meet the president's definition, terrorism experts say. Moreover, in June 2002, Singapore accused Hezbollah of recruiting Singaporeans in a failed 1990s plot to attack US and Israeli ships in the Singapore Straits. In November 2001 the State Department placed Hezbollah on a formal list of foreign terrorist organizations whose financial assets can be seized.

Does Hezbollah have any ties to al-Qaeda? Yes, although the Shiite clerics who rule Iran have a different radical religious outlook than those of the Sunni Muslims of both the al-Qaeda terrorist network and the Taliban, which targeted Shiites in Afghanistan. But Mugniyah did reportedly meet at least once during the 1990s with bin Laden. Moreover, Hezbollah and al-Qaeda have reportedly been cooperating on logistics and training for some operations, according to intelligence officials and some terrorism experts. How did Hezbollah react to 9/11? The group's spiritual leader, Sheikh Muhammad Hussein Fadlallah, condemned the attacks as incompatible with Islamic law and perversions of the true meaning of *jihad.* Fadlallah accuses bin Laden of heeding "personal psychological needs" and calls the hijackers "merely suicides"—rather than martyrs—because they killed innocent civilians.

Hezbollah is active in politics and has 12 seats in Lebanon's 128-member parliament, which is elected in a system that experts say tends to magnify the influence of Christian and Sunni groups worried about Shiite influence over the country. The group entered the Lebanese political arena after Lebanon's civil war ended in 1990 and the country fell under Syrian influence.

Jemaah Islamiyah (JI): JI is a militant Islamist group active in several Southeast Asian countries that is seeking to establish a Muslim fundamentalist state in the region.

The name Jemaah Islamiyah dates to the late 1970s, but experts are not certain if the name referred to a formal organization or an informal gathering of like-minded Muslim radicals— or a government label for Islamist malcontents. The group has its roots in Darul Islam, a violent radical movement that advocated the establishment of Islamic law in Indonesia, the world's most populous Muslim country and also home to Christians, Hindus, and adherents of other faiths. Darul Islam sprang up as the country emerged from Dutch colonial rule in the late 1940s, and it continued to resist the postcolonial Indonesian republic, which it saw as too secular.

Abu Bakar Bashir, an Indonesian of Yemeni decent, is thought to be the group's spiritual leader—and, some speculate, an operational leader as well. Bashir joined Darul Islam in the 1970s and was imprisoned in Indonesia for Islamist activism. In 1985 after a court ordered him back to prison, Bashir fled to Malaysia. There, he recruited volunteers to fight in the anti-Soviet Muslim brigades in Afghanistan and sought funding from Saudi Arabia while maintaining connections with former colleagues in Indonesia. Antiterror authorities struck a blow against JI when they arrested its operational chief, Nurjaman Riduan Ismuddin (aka Hambali), in Thailand in mid-August 2003.

JI operates across Southeast Asia, including Indonesia, Malaysia, Singapore and, possibly, the Philippines and Thailand. Weak central authority, lax or corrupt law enforcement, and open maritime borders in some of these countries ease JI's ability to operate throughout the region. The group—or individuals affiliated with it—is thought to be tied to several terrorist plots. Among them are the following:

The August 2003 car bombing of the J. W. Marriott Hotel in Jakarta that killed 12 people.

- The October 2002 bombing of a nightclub on the predominantly Hindu island of Bali that killed 202 people, most of them foreign tourists from Australia and elsewhere. Amrozi bin Nurhasyim, a 41-year-old mechanic from east Java, was convicted on 8 August for buying the vehicle used in the main explosion and buying and transporting most of the chemicals used for the explosives. He was the first of 33 suspects arrested for the bombings to be convicted.

- A December 2000 wave of church bombings in Indonesia that killed 18. Asian and US officials say Hambali had a hand in these attacks, and Indonesian officials arrested JI leader Bashir for questioning in connection with this anti-Christian campaign.

- A December 2000 series of bombings in Manila that killed 22. The State Department says Hambali helped plan these attacks. Fathur Rahman al-Ghozi, a Bashir follower, reportedly confessed to a role in the bombings. In April 2002 he was convicted in the Philippines on unrelated charges of possessing explosives.

- A 1995 plot to bomb 11 US commercial airliners in Asia that, the State Department says, Hambali helped plan.

After the Bali attack, the United States—which suspects the group of having ties to Osama bin Laden's al-Qaeda network—

designated JI a foreign terrorist organization. JI has also been linked to aborted plans to attack US, British, and Australian embassies in Singapore.

Does JI have links to al-Qaeda? Probably, but experts disagree on the extent of them. Some US officials and terrorism experts suspect that JI is a subdivision of al-Qaeda capable of opening a second front against US interests in Southeast Asia. Other experts argue that the two are not that closely linked and add that Jemaah Islamiyah's regional goals do not fully match al-Qaeda's global aspirations. Bashir denies the group has ties to al-Qaeda, but he has expressed support for Osama bin Laden. An al-Qaeda operative arrested in Indonesia reportedly told US investigators that Bashir was directly involved in al-Qaeda plots. At the very least, a few individuals have been linked to both groups. Hambali is the JI leader thought to be most closely linked to al-Qaeda. He allegedly has been involved in several terrorist attacks and plots in the region.

Glossary

ASG	Abu Sayyaf Group
BOC	Balkan Organized Crime
CD	compact disc
CIA	Central Intelligence Agency
DEA	Drug Enforcement Administration
DOJ	Department of Justice
DVD	digital video disc (now digital versatile disc)
FARC	Revolutionary Armed Forces of Colombia
FATF	Financial Action Task Force
FBI	Federal Bureau of Investigation
FinCEN	Financial Crimes Enforcement Network
GAO	General Accounting Office
GKN	State Committee for the Control of Narcotics and Psychotropic Substances
GRECO	Council of Europe's Group of States against Corruption
G-7/8	The G-7/8 countries are the United States, Britain, Canada, Italy, Germany, France, and Japan; Russia is the eighth member
ILEA	International Law Enforcement Academies
INL	Bureau of International Narcotics and Law Enforcement Affairs, State Department
IOC	Italian Organized Crime
IRS	Internal Revenue Service
JI	Jemaah Islamiyah
LCN	La Cosa Nostra
MLAT	mutual legal assistance treaties
OPDAT	Office of Overseas Prosecutorial Development, Assistance and Training
UN	United Nations
USA PATRIOT	Uniting and Strengthening America by Providing Appropriate Tools Required to Intercept and Obstruct Terrorism Act

Bibliography

Al-Haramain Foundation. "Al-Haramain Was Shut Down by the Saudi Government because of a Charge of Funding Islamic Terrorism." 6 Oct 2004. http://www.answering-islam.org/Responses/Alharamain/.

Anderson, Curt. "Terror Investigators Raid Mass. Company." *Financial News*, 6 Dec 2002.

Annan, Kofi. "UN Statement on Convention against Organized Crime." Palermo, Italy, 12 Dec 2000. http://www.unodc.org/unodc/speech_2000-12-12_1.html.

Arab Press. "The Role of Fatwas in Incitement to Terrorism." 18 Jan 2002. http://www.ourjerusalem.com/arabpress/story/arabpress20020120.html.

Ashley, Grant D. "Transnational Organized Crime." In Subcommittee on European Affairs, US Senate, Committee on Foreign Relations. *Congressional Testimony.* 108th Cong., 1st sess., 30 Oct 2003.

Asian-Nation, The Landscape of Asian America. "Asian-American Gangs." http://www.asian-nation.org/gangs.shtml.

Aversa, Jeannine. "Nations to Discuss Ways to Cut Off Terrorists' Financing." *Associated Press*, 4 Feb 2004.

———. "U.S. to Sharpen Focus on Terror Funding." *Associated Press Online*, 19 Nov 2003. http://www.ap.org/.

Berniker, Mark. "Afghanistan Stands on Brink of Becoming 'Narco-State.'" *Eurasia Insight*, 26 Mar 2004.

Brisard, Jean-Charles. *Terrorism Financing: Roots and Trends of Saudi Terrorism Financing.* 19 Dec 2002. http://www.nationalreview.com/document/document-un/22002.pdf.

Bush, George W. "Executive Order on Terrorist Financing: Blocking Property and Prohibiting Transactions with Persons Who Commit, Threaten to Commit, or Support Terrorism." 24 Sept 2001. http://www.whitehouse.gov/news/releases/2001/09/20010924-1.html.

———. "Statement of the President, 14 Dec 2001." http://www.whitehouse.gov/news/releases/2001/12/20011214-2.html.

77

Center for Strategic and International Studies (CSIS). "Canadian Agency Finds Dirty Money." 13 Sept 2003. http://www.csis.org/tnt/ttu/ttu_0309.pdf.

———. "Transnational Threats Update." December 2003. http://www.csis.org/tnt/ttu/ttu_0312.pdf.

Cilluffo, Frank. "The Threat Posed from the Convergence of Organized Crime, Drug Trafficking, and Terrorism." In House, Committee on the Judiciary. *Congressional Testimony.* 106th Cong., 2d sess., 13 Dec 2000.

Clark, Richard. "The Financing of Terror Organizations." In US Senate, Banking, Housing, and Urban Affairs Committee. *Congressional Testimony.* 108th Cong., 1st sess., 23 Oct 2003. http://banking.senate.gov/_files/clarke.pdf.

Council on Foreign Relations. "Are Terrorists in Colombia?" 2004. http://www.terrorismanswers.com/groups/farc.html#Q2.

Cowell, Alan. "45 Nations Set to Back Rules on Illicit Diamond Trading." *New York Times,* 3 Nov 2002.

———. "Terrorism's Cost in a Global Economy." *New York Times,* 9 Nov 2003.

Denny, David A. *Terrorism, Drug Trafficking Inextricably Linked, US Experts Say.* Washington, D.C.: Drug Enforcement Agency, 5 Dec 2001.

Department of State. "Bureau for International Narcotics and Law Enforcement Affairs." 2004. http://www.state.gov/g/inl/.

———. "Trafficking in Persons Report." 11 June 2003. http://www.state.gov/g/tip/rls/tiprpt/2003/21262.htm#tiers.

———. "Victims of Trafficking and Violence Protection Act of 2000." Sept 2003. http://www.immigrationlinks.com/news/news1184.htm3.

Departments of Treasury and Justice. "2003 National Money Laundering Strategy." http://www.ustreas.gov/press/releases/reports/js10102.pdf.

Dilanian, Ken. "U.N. Report Finds Two Terror Financiers Living, Doing Business Freely." Knight-Ridder News Service, 5 Dec 2003.

Drug Enforcement Administration. "Drugs and Terror: Under-
    standing the Link and the Impact on America." 2004.
    http://www.theantidrug.com.
"Drug Ring Linked to Terror." *Detroit Free Press*, 2 Sept 2002.
Farah, Douglas. "Report Says Africans Harbored al-Qaeda: Ter-
    ror Assets Hidden in Gem-Buying Spree." *Washington Post*,
    29 Dec 2002.
———. "Syria Seizes Six Arab Couriers, $23 Million." *Washington
    Post*, 20 Dec 2003.
———. "Terrorism Inc.: Al-Qaeda Franchises Brand of Violence
    to Groups across World." *Washington Post*, 21 Nov 2003.
"Federal Reserve Examiner Spreads Knowledge to Global Au-
    dience." *Alert Global Media, Inc.*, 2003.
Financial Action Task Force on Money Laundering. "What Is
    Money Laundering?" 10 Sept 2003. http://www1.oecd.
    org/fatf/index.htm.
"Fraud, ID Theft Finance Terror." *Chicago Tribune*, 4 Nov 2001.
General Accounting Office (GAO). "Combating Terrorism: In-
    teragency Framework and Agency Program to Address the
    Overseas Threat." 23 May 2003. http://www.gao.gov/
    new.items/d03165.pdf.
———. "Federal Agencies Face Continuing Challenges in Ad-
    dressing Terrorist Financing and Money Laundering." 4
    Mar 2004. http://www.gao.gov/new.items/d04501t.pdf.
———. "Terrorist Financing: US Agencies Should Systematically
    Assess Terrorists' Use of Alternative Financing Mecha-
    nisms." 14 Nov 2003. http://www.gao.gov/new.items/
    d04163.pdf.
Global Business Consulting Incorporated's (GBCI) Official Web
    Site. "Welcome to GBCI." http://www.gbci.net.
*Global Relief Foundation, Inc. v. Paul H. O'Neill, Colin L. Powell,
    John Ashcroft, R. Richard Newcomb, and Robert S. Mueller III.*
    In *US District Court, Northern District of Illinois*. 11 June 2002.
    http://news.findlaw.com/hdocs/docs/terrorism/bifash
    croft013002cmp.pdf.
National Security Council. "Champion Aspirations for Human
    Dignity." 1 June 2002. http://www.whitehouse.gov/nsc/
    nss2.html.

Noble, Ronald K. "The Links between Intellectual Property Crime and Terrorist Financing." In US House, Committee on International Relations. *Congressional Testimony*. 108th Cong., 1st sess., 16 July 2003. http://www.interpol.int/Public/ICPO/speeches/SG20030716.asp.

O'Harrow, Robert, Jr. "Identity Crisis: Meet Michael Berry: Political Activist, Cancer Survivor, Creditor's Dream. Meet Michael Berry: Scam Artist, Killer, the Real Michael Berry's Worst Nightmare." *Washington Post*, 10 Aug 2003, 14–29.

Pifer, Steven. "Combating Transnational Crime and Corruption in Europe." In US Senate, Foreign Relations Committee. *Congressional Testimony*. 108th Cong., 1st sess., 10 Oct 2003. http://foreign.senate.gov/testimony/2003/PiferTestimony031030.pdf.

Scarborough, Rowan. "Drug Money Sustains al-Qaeda." *Washington Times*, 29 Dec 2003.

Schrage, Steve. "Combating Transnational Crime and Corruption in Europe." In US Senate, Committee on Foreign Relations, Subcommittee on European Affairs. 108th Cong., 1st sess., 30 Oct 2003. http://www.state.gov/g/inl/rls/rm/25755.htm.

Seper, Jerry. "US Agents Raid Software Firm, Seeking al-Qaeda Money Link." *Washington Times*, 7 Dec 2002, 2.

"Treasury Revokes Tax-Exempt Status of 3 Muslim Charities." *Associated Press*, 14 Nov 2003.

United States of America v. Enaam M. Arnaout. In *United States District Court, Northern District of Illinois*. 2002. http://www.usdoj.gov/usao/iln/indict/2002/02cr892.pdf.

United States of America v. Zacarias Moussaoui. In *United States District Court, Eastern Division of Virginia*. 14 July 2003. http://www.usdoj.gov/ag/moussaouiindictment.htm.

Vistica, Gregory. "Frozen Assets Going to Legal Bills: US Has Linked Confiscated Funds to Financing Terror." *Washington Post*, 2 Nov 2003.

Waller, J. Michael. "D. C. Islamist Agent Carried Libyan Cash." *News World Communications, Inc.*, 10 Nov 2003.

Wikipedia. *The Free Encyclopedia*. English edition, Jan 2001. http:///en.wikipedia.org/wiki/Main_Page.

Transnational Crime and the Criminal-Terrorist Nexus

Synergies and Corporate Trends

Air University Press Team

Chief Editor
Emily J. Adams

Copy Editor
Sherry Terrell

Book Design and Cover Art
Steven C. Garst

*Composition and
Prepress Production*
Mary P. Ferguson

Quality Review
Mary J. Moore

Print Preparation
Joan Hickey

Distribution
Diane Clark

www.ingramcontent.com/pod-product-compliance
Lightning Source LLC
Chambersburg PA
CBHW082142290526
45794CB00008B/3138